15 Days of Prayer
With Charles de Foucauld

D1502144

Also in this collection:

André Dupleix
15 Days of Prayer
With Pierre Teilhard de Chardin

André Gozier
15 Days of Prayer
With Thomas Merton

Constant Tonnelier
15 Days of Prayer
With Saint Thérèse of Lisieux

François Vayne
15 Days of Prayer
With Saint Bernadette of Lourdes

15 DAYS OF PRAYER

WITH

Charles
de Foucauld

MICHEL LAFON

Translated by Victoria Hébert and Denis Sabourin

Liguori
LIGUORI, MISSOURI

Liguori, Missouri
http://www.liguori.org

This book is a translation of *Prier 15 Jours Avec Charles de Foucauld*, published by Nouvelle Cité, 1995, Montrouge, France.

Library of Congress Cataloging-in-Publication Data

Lafon, Michel, père.
    [Prier 15 jours avec Charles de Foucauld. English]
    15 days of prayer with Charles de Foucauld / Michel Lafon ; translated by Victoria Hébert and Denis Sabourin. — 1st English ed.
        p.   cm.
    Includes bibliographical references.
    ISBN 0-7648-0489-8 (pbk.)
    1. Foucauld, Charles de, 1858–1916 Meditations. 2. Spiritual life— Catholic Church. I. Title. II. Title: Fifteen days of prayer with Charles de Foucauld.
BX4705.F65L3213 1999
269'.6—dc21   99-34425

Printed in the United States of America
03 02 01 00 99   5 4 3 2 1
First English Edition 1999

Table of Contents

How to Use This Book

AN OLD CHINESE PROVERB, or at least what I am able to recall of what is supposed to be an old Chinese proverb, goes something like this: "Even a journey of a thousand miles begins with a single step." When you think about it, the truth of the proverb is obvious. It is impossible to begin any project, let alone a journey, without taking the first step. I think it might also be true, although I cannot recall if another Chinese proverb says it, "that the first step is often the hardest." Or, as someone else once observed, "the distance between a thought and the corresponding action needed to implement the idea takes the most energy." I don't know who shared that perception with me but I am certain it was not an old Chinese master!

With this ancient proverbial wisdom, and the not-so-ancient wisdom of an unknown contemporary sage still fresh, we move from proverbs to presumptions. How do these relate to the task before us?

I am presuming that if you are reading this introduction it is because you are contemplating a journey. My presumption is that you are preparing for a spiritual journey and that you have taken at least some of the first steps necessary to prepare for this journey. I also presume, and please excuse me if I am making too many presumptions, that in your preparation for the spiritual journey you have determined that you need a guide. From deep within the recesses of your deepest self, there was something that called you to consider Charles de Foucauld as a potential companion. If my presumptions are correct, may I congratulate you on this decision? I think you have made a wise choice, a choice that can be confirmed by yet another source of wisdom, the wisdom that comes from practical experience.

Even an informal poll of experienced travelers will reveal a common opinion; it is very difficult to travel alone. Some might observe that it is even foolish. Still others may be even stronger in their opinion and go so far as to insist that it is necessary to have a guide, especially when you are traveling into uncharted waters and into territory that you have not yet experienced. I am of the personal opinion that a traveling companion is welcome under all circumstances. The thought of traveling alone, to some exciting destination without someone to share the journey with does not capture my imagination or channel my enthusiasm. However, with that being noted, what is simply a matter of preference on the normal journey becomes a matter of necessity when a person embarks on a spiritual journey.

The spiritual journey, which can be the most challenging of all journeys, is experienced best with a guide, a companion, or at the very least, a friend in whom you have placed your trust. This observation is not a preference or an opinion but rather an established spiritual necessity. All of the great saints with whom I am familiar had a spiritual director or a confessor who journeyed with them. Admittedly, at times the saint might well have traveled far beyond the experience of their guide and companion but more often than not they would return to their director and reflect on their experience. Understood in this sense, the director and companion provided a valuable contribution and necessary resource.

When I was learning how to pray (a necessity for anyone who desires to be a full-time and public "religious person"), the community of men that I belong to gave me a great gift. Between my second and third year in college, I was given a one-year sabbatical, with all expenses paid and all of my personal needs met. This period of time was called novitiate. I was officially designated as a novice, a beginner in the spiritual journey, and I was assigned a "master," a person who was willing to lead me. In addition to the master, I was provided with every imaginable book and any other resource that I could possibly need. Even with all that I was provided, I did not learn how to pray because of the books and the unlimited resources, rather it was the master, the companion who was the key to the experience.

One day, after about three months of reading, of quiet and solitude, and of practicing all of the methods and descriptions of prayer that were available to me, the master called. "Put away the books, forget the method, and just listen." We went into a room, became quiet, and tried to recall the presence of God, and then, the master simply prayed out loud and permitted me to listen to his prayer. As he prayed, he revealed his hopes, his dreams, his struggles, his successes, and most of all, his relationship with God. I discovered as I listened that his prayer was deeply intimate but most of all it was self-revealing. As I learned about him, I was led through his life experience to the place where God dwells. At that moment I was able to understand a little bit about what I was supposed to do if I really wanted to pray.

The dynamic of what happened when the master called, invited me to listen, and then revealed his innermost self to me as he communicated with God in prayer, was important. It wasn't so much that the master was trying to reveal to me what needed to be said; he was not inviting me to pray with the same words that he used, but rather that he was trying to bring me to that place within myself where prayer becomes possible. That place, a place of intimacy and of self-awareness, was a necessary stop on the journey and it was a place that I needed to be led to. I could not have easily discovered it on my own.

The purpose of the volume that you hold in your hand is to lead you, over a period of fifteen days or, maybe more realistically, fifteen prayer periods, to a place where prayer is possible. If you already have a regular experience and practice of prayer, perhaps this volume can help lead you to a deeper place, a more intimate relationship with the Lord.

It is important to note that the purpose of this book is not to lead you to a better relationship with Charles de Foucauld, your spiritual companion. Although your companion will invite you to share some of their deepest and most intimate thoughts, your companion is doing so only to bring you to that place where God dwells. After all, the true measurement of a companion for the journey is that they bring you to the place where you need to be, and then they step back, out of the picture. A guide who brings you to the desired destination and then sticks around is a very unwelcome guest!

Many times I have found myself attracted to a particular idea or method for accomplishing a task, only to discover that what seemed to be inviting and helpful possessed too many details. All of my energy went to the mastery of the details and I soon lost my enthusiasm. In each instance, the book that seemed so promising ended up on my bookshelf, gathering dust. I can assure you, it is not our intention that this book end up in your bookcase, filled with promise, but unable to deliver.

There are three simple rules that need to be followed in order to use this book with a measure of satisfaction.

Place: It is important that you choose a place for reading that provides the necessary atmosphere for reflection and that does not allow for too many distractions. Whatever place you choose needs to be comfortable, have the necessary lighting, and, finally, have a sense of "welcoming" about it. You need to be able to look forward to the experience of the journey. Don't travel steerage if you know you will be more comfortable in first class and if the choice is realistic for you. On the other hand, if first class is a distraction and you feel more comfortable and more yourself in steerage, then it is in steerage that you belong.

My favorite place is an overstuffed and comfortable chair in my bedroom. There is a light over my shoulder, and the chair reclines if I feel a need to recline. Once in a while, I get lucky and the sun comes through my window and bathes the entire room in light. I have other options and other places that are available to me but this is the place that I prefer.

Time: Choose a time during the day when you are most alert and when you are most receptive to reflection, meditation, and prayer. The time that you choose is an essential component. If you are a morning person, for example, you should choose a time that is in the morning. If you are more alert in the afternoon, choose an afternoon time slot; and if evening is your preference, then by all means choose the evening. Try to avoid "peak" periods in your daily routine when you know that you might be disturbed. The time that you choose needs to be your time and needs to work for you.

It is also important that you choose how much time you will spend with your companion each day. For some it will be possible to set aside enough time in order to read and reflect on all the material that is offered for a given day. For others, it might not be possible to devote one time to the suggested material for the day, so the prayer period may need to be extended for two, three, or even more sessions. It is not important how long it takes you; it is only important that it works for you and that you remain committed to that which is possible.

For myself I have found that fifteen minutes in the early morning, while I am still in my robe and pajamas and before my morning coffee, and even before I prepare myself for the day, is the best time. No one expects to see me or to interact with me because I have not yet "announced" the fact that I am awake or even on the move. However, once someone hears me in the bathroom, then my window of opportunity is gone. It is therefore important to me that I use the time that I have identified when it is available to me.

Freedom: It may seem strange to suggest that freedom is the third necessary ingredient, but I have discovered that it is most important. By freedom I understand a certain "stance toward life," a "permission to be myself and to be gentle and understanding of who I am." I am constantly amazed at how the human person so easily sets himself or herself up for disappointment and perceived failure. We so easily make judgments about ourselves and our actions and our choices, and very often those judgments are negative, and not at all helpful.

For instance, what does it really matter if I have chosen a

place and a time, and I have missed both the place and the time for three days in a row? What does it matter if I have chosen, in that twilight time before I am completely awake and still a little sleepy, to roll over and to sleep for fifteen minutes more? Does it mean that I am not serious about the journey, that I really don't want to pray, that I am just fooling myself when I say that my prayer time is important to me? Perhaps, but I prefer to believe that it simply means that I am tired and I just wanted a little more sleep. It doesn't mean anything more than that. However, if I make it mean more than that, then I can become discouraged, frustrated, and put myself into a state where I might more easily give up. "What's the use? I might as well forget all about it."

The same sense of freedom applies to the reading and the praying of this text. If I do not find the introduction to each day helpful, I don't need to read it. If I find the questions for reflection at the end of the appointed day repetitive, then I should choose to close the book and go my own way. Even if I discover that the reflection offered for the day is not the one that I prefer and that the one for the next day seems more inviting, then by all means, go on to the one for the next day.

That's it! If you apply these simple rules to your journey you should receive the maximum benefit and you will soon find yourself at your destination. But be prepared to be surprised. If you have never been on a spiritual journey you should know that the "travel brochures" and the other descriptions that you might have heard are nothing compared to the real thing. There is so much more than you can imagine.

A final prayer of blessing suggests itself:

> Lord, catch me off guard today.
> Surprise me with some moment of beauty
>   or pain
> So that at least for the moment
> I may be startled into seeing that you are here
>   in all your splendor,
> Always and everywhere,
> Barely hidden,
> Beneath,
> Beyond,
> Within this life I breathe.

—Frederick Buechner

REV. THOMAS M. SANTA, CSsR
LIGUORI, MISSOURI
FEAST OF THE PRESENTATION, 1999

A Brief Chronology
of Charles de Foucauld's Life

HERE ARE THE IMPORTANT DATES in Charles de Foucauld's life. This chronology will permit the reader to situate the texts and follow the evolution of his life during the fifteen days of the spiritual journey outlined in this book.

September 15, 1858:

    Charles de Foucauld was born in Strasbourg, France.

1864: He was orphaned at the age of six and entrusted to the care of his maternal grandparents. The war of 1870–71 forced the family to flee and settle in Nancy.

1876: Charles entered school at Saint–Cyr, and then studied at the cavalry school in Saumur. In possession of a large fortune, he lived a life of revelry and dissipation.

1878: He received a commission as a second lieutenant in the French army.

1880: His regiment, which was garrisoned at Pont-à-Mousson, was sent to Setif in Algeria. Charles appears in public with his mistress and is discharged. He is reinstated and, with his comrades, participates in a campaign in the south of Oran. He recognized that his "faith had been completely dead for twelve years."

1883–1884:

Having left the army again, he explored Morocco, disguised as the Jewish servant of a rabbi. Upon his return, he wrote a book about his travels and received a gold medal from the Geography Society of Paris. He lived in Algiers, then Paris.

October, 1886:

At St. Augustine Church (Paris), he "converted" at the hands of Abbé Henri Huvelin, who became his spiritual guide. He made a pilgrimage to the Holy Land.

1890–1896:

He entered the Trappists at Notre Dames des Neiges (Ardèche) at Nazareth and took the name Brother Marie-Albéric. Then, he left for the Trappists of Akbès in Syria.

January, 1897:

In Rome, the Father General of the Trappists released Charles de Foucauld from his vows and authorized him "to follow his vocation." He worked as a servant with the Clarists in Nazareth for four years. It was during this period that he wrote the majority of his meditations.

June 9, 1901:

He was ordained a priest at Viviers and decided to leave for the Sahara, to be "among the lambs who were the most neglected." He took up residence in Beni-Abbès on the Morocco-Algeria frontier.

1904–1905:

Accompanying the military, he visited the southern oases of the Sahara and went all the way to the Tuaregs in Hoggar. He took up residence with them in Tamanrasset. But, as he was alone, he was forced to divide his time between Beni-Abbès and Tamanrasset.

1907–1908:

Second stay in Hoggar.

1909: Trip to France.

1910–1915:

He returned to Tamanrasset, where he remained until his death, with the exception of two trips to France in 1911 and in 1913. During these years, he devoted a great deal of his time to linguistic works: dictionaries, collections of poetry, and so on, in the Tuareg language.

1916: The Djanet fort, which protected the eastern border, fell into the hands of the Sensi sect of Libya. A small fort was built in Tamanrasset to protect the population in the event of dire circumstances. Charles moved there.

December 1, 1916:

Charles died, assassinated by a group of Tuareg Senoussistes.

Introduction

"Live closely with a great saint and a great spirit, your heart will become warm like his, your faith alive like his, your spirit will arise in the same way as his."

Charles de Foucauld

TO WANT TO PRAY with a saint of any stature—do greater and lesser ones even exist?—makes us penetrate into his spiritual universe and makes us discover the sources of his life. This discovery is possible because life penetrates prayer like it inspires our behavior. I hope that this choice of texts written by Charles de Foucauld and the commentary about them will be able to assist you, not only to pray, but also (at the risk of disagreeing with the title of this collection) to live—and to live beyond our fifteen days together!

Essential support for the meditation and prayer which form the very substance of the journey on which we are about to embark is found in the texts written by Charles de Foucauld. These selections have been chosen from his very large number of writings because they have struck me as significant and as well connected to the Gospel; that is to say, they fit with a particular teaching of our Lord Jesus which I have chosen for each day. Through my comments, I simply want to further explain and elaborate on Father de Foucauld's meditation, without being so presumptuous as to put myself in his place: the "I" that I have used refers both to myself and to you, as I try to pray with you in the light of the selected message for each of the fifteen days. I did not seek to propose a "all-purpose" prayer, but rather to provide material so that you may create your own. I hope that the many extracts from Brother Charles's prayers will be appropriate for our journey together.

Here is a preview of the progression of the fifteen days. The starting point for journey to conversion with Father de Foucauld is to recognize that God is absolute and that our only desire is to live only for him (Day 1). In doing so, we must rejoice in his happiness (Day 2); do our best to imitate the Beloved Jesus of Our Father (Day 3); and follow, in particular, his poverty (Day 4).

Then we are invited to go from an exterior Christ to a Christ who lives within us (Day 5), for whom we are witnesses (Day 6) through sharing the life of our brothers (Day 7). In us and through us, Jesus wants to continue to save our brothers (Day 8) and love them (Day 9).

Our love cannot be expressed in words: obedience is the cornerstone (Day 10), and it expresses itself in our prayers (Day 11), whose summit is the intimate unity in the Eucharist (Day 12), where Jesus gives himself to us (Day 13). Our death is an act of total abandonment and confident love, as our life will have been (Days 14 and 15).

Even though the preceding description presents a seemingly discrete picture and each day appears autonomous, a certain theme started in one place may also be developed later. A certain paragraph in one day's meditation may complete a comment from a previous day. These crossovers, these repetitions, only prove just how much everything revolves around a few very simple streams of thought, which I hope you will easily discover and which converge into what the Little Brothers of Tamanrasset's red emblem proclaims: the heart and the cross, framed by the two sacred names: Jesus Caritas. In any case, there is one word which we cannot ignore, either in citing Foucauld's texts or in offering our commentary. This word is the verb "to love," which we proclaim in every tense. Isn't this word itself what unified the life of the one who, according to Father Huvelin, "turned religion into love"?

I would also like to make a few remarks to assist your understanding in the pages that follow:

1. I have made a few modifications to Charles de Foucauld's texts (I think he would allow it), by using a more familiar word to refer to God. This brotherly salutation is presently in common use in liturgy and personal prayer, especially since Vatican II.

2. I have shortened the length of Father de Foucauld's texts, which I have not always indicated. I took the liberty of shortening these texts in order to better underline their principal ideas. Since the source of the texts are clearly given— even if the presence of these sources weighs the comments down a bit—some of you who want to may easily refer to the original text itself. One note, however: the majority of the ellipses in the texts are from Father de Foucauld himself; this was a mark of his writing style and his way of expressing himself.

3. In this book, I have found it simpler to refer to our spiritual guide as "Brother Charles."

4. May our female readers forgive my generalized use of the masculine, but old habits are hard to break!

Finally, as well as asking you to attentively read this modest book, may I ask you, dear readers, to include prayers for my own conversion with your own prayers? Thank you.

MICHEL LAFON,
EL KBAB, APRIL 1995

Abbreviations Used in This Book

HERE ARE DESCRIPTIONS of each abbreviation and citation found in parentheses at the end of the quotations in this book. In each parentheses, the number that follows the abbreviation will indicate the page from which the excerpt is taken, with the exception of MSE, where it will indicate the number of the meditation.

B   *Charles de Foucauld, Explorateur du Maroc, Eremite au Sahara* by René Bazin, Plon, Paris, 1921.

ES   *Écrit spirituels* (Spiritual Writings) compiled by René Bazin, Paris: De Gigord, 1958.

OS   *Frère Charles de Jésus, Oeuvres Spirituelles: Anthologie* edited by René Bazin. Paris: Seuil, 1958.

Correspondence:

LFT   Letters to my Trappist Brothers, Paris: Cerf, 1991.

LGT   Letters to a high school friend (Gabriel Tourdes), Paris: Nouvelle Cité, 1982.

LHC   Letters to Henry de Castries, Paris: Grasset, 1938.

LLM Letters to Louis Massignon, Paris: Seuil, 1993.

LMB Letters to Madame de Bondy, Paris: Desclée, 1966.

Spiritual Works (*Oeuvres Spirituelles*, by Charles de Foucauld, in 15 Volumes, Nouvelle Cité):

CB   Beni-Abbès Workbook

CE   Proclaim the Gospel

CFA   Thoughts About the Feast Days of the Year

CM   Comments About Saint Matthew

CT   Tamanrasset Workbook

DP   The Last Place

EDS   One God

EJ   Jesus' Spirit

MSE   Meditations on the Holy Gospels

PFJ   Little Brother of Jesus

PPF   To the Smallest of My Brothers

QPR   Who Could Resist God

RD   Rules and Directory

SAD   Alone With God

VN   Night Traveler

15 Days of Prayer
With Charles de Foucauld

DAY ONE

Live for God Alone

FOCUS POINT

Our Christian call is a journey to live our lives for God alone. We are called to empty ourselves so that we might be filled with God. This process of allowing God to fill us with the mystery of Jesus opens our eyes, heart, and mind to the fullness of the first commandment: "To love God with our whole heart, mind, and soul and our neighbor as ourselves."

As soon as I believed that there was a God, I understood that I could do nothing else but live only for him. My vocation came at the very same time as my faith. God is so great! There is such a vast difference between God and all that is not him (LHC, 96).

May our only treasure be God, may our heart belong totally to God, everything in God, everything for God…for him alone.

Let us be emptied of everything, everything that is creation, even detached from spiritual goods, even God's graces, emptied of everything...so that we may be completely filled with God. (...) He has the right to it all, our entire heart. We keep it all for him, all of everything for him alone (PFJ, 89).

The eyes which I found to be the gentlest, the smiles which consoled me the most, the people who captivated me the most, all of this was only but a small part of your beauty that you let me see, so that by seeing these things, I could say: that comes from God. (...) My God, how good you are to have shown me your beauty through your creations! Give me the grace to see only you in creation....Allow me to see through the veils...(DP, 38–39).

Every time I open a window or a door, I am ecstatic when I see the mountain peaks that surround me and which I oversee. It is a marvelous sight and a scene of truly beautiful solitude. How good it makes me feel in this great calm and beautiful, yet tormented and strange, scene to lift up my heart toward the Creator and the Savior, Jesus! (LMB, 200).

L ord Jesus, I see you standing in front of the Temple with the outline of its columns behind you. Before you stands this scribe of good faith who questions you, saying "Which commandment is the first of all?" The circle of listeners are silent. Then you answer, O Jesus, and may your response echo in me as if you are speaking to me today for the very first time: "Hear, O Israel: the Lord our God, the Lord is one; you shall love the Lord your God with all your heart, and with all your soul, and with all your mind, and with all your strength" (Mk 12:29–30). Then you add, with the same passion: "You shall love your neighbor as yourself. There is no other commandment greater than these" (Mk 12:31).

Of the disputatious scribes, one agreed with Jesus and answered affirmatively. His answer strikes me: it testifies to the faith of a true worshiper of a single, unique God—a worship which is not, as such, exclusive to Christians. The scribe answers: "You are right, Teacher; you have truly said that 'he is one, and besides him there is no other'" (Mk 12:32).

I see this scribe as a spokesperson for millions and millions of Muslims who have, for many centuries, repeated what he said, this same profession of faith in the first part of the *shahada:* "I bear witness that there is no god but God" (*la ilaha illa Allah*). Is it not moving then, Lord Jesus, to hear yourself say to this scribe—and through him, to the crowds of believers: "You are not far from the kingdom of God" (Mk 12:34)? This way, Jews, Christians, and Muslims, we all recognize ourselves as brothers through Jesus' own formula—itself taken from a verse in Deuteronomy. We are truly the children of Abraham, the believer, "for he is the father of all of us" (Rom 4:16).

Was the religious testimony of the Muslims not the starting point of the road that took Brother Charles to his conversion? He admitted that "Islam produced a great upheaval within me....The view of this faith, of these souls living in the continuous presence of God, made me catch a glimpse of something even greater and truer than mundane concerns" (LHC, 86).

The cry "Allah Akbar," thousands of times exclaimed from the heights of the minarets or repeated by the prostrated believers, condenses the deep Muslim sentiment regarding humans and events: "Allah Akbar, God is greater than anything we could imagine. Only he, above all, deserves our thoughts and words" (LHC, 94).

Could the Muslims who have been placed on my road be witness to an uncompromising faith in the grandeur of God? And can this witness stimulate my own understanding of the transcendence of God? Is God not the One and Only for me as well? "O You, above all others," the liturgy sings in me. Am I not too used to a God who is near, familiar, and friendly? Have I not diminished the meaning of the mystery of God in my spirit? Can I share Brother Charles's feelings about this: "For me, everything is overshadowed by the happiness of knowing that God is God, by the thanksgiving for his great glory" (LHC, 157)?

It seems as if Jesus is saying to me: "This scribe has replied with faith, but you, what is your answer?" Oh, how that question must express the wish for a total commitment, especially when I hear you, Lord Jesus, stress the word "all"—this "all" that Brother Charles does not stop repeating—with *all* my heart, with *all* my soul, with *all* my spirit, with *all* my strength. Yes, my God, with all of myself, all my desires, all my faith, I recognize you, I adore you, I give you thanks. "I believe; help my unbelief!" (Mk 9:24).

I prostrate myself before this invisible God. When I arise, I must not close my eyes because that is when he gives me a sign. Do not the splendors of creation and humanity speak to me about him? A marvelous sunset, a smile, a beautiful glance, an act of true kindness: are not all of these a reflection of his light, his divine brilliance?

How can I experience these splendors and not hear the silent words? Lord, you are too quiet: has no one ever told you that? Also, I am undoubtedly too caught up in the world around me and in my own activities to be able to hear beyond what my ears hear and see beyond what my eyes see.

To love you, O my God, gives place to the only absolute. No matter what my vocation, the rest is measured in the light of this fundamental conviction: "In this way, whoever lives in faith has a soul filled with new thoughts, new tastes, and new judgments. These are new horizons which open before him, enlightened by a heavenly light. (...) Necessarily, that person begins a completely new life, one which goes against a world to which these actions seem foolish" (DP, 120).

These phrases echo what Brother Charles felt following his conversion. A new life began for him; a life whose goal was "to live only for God." Is that not the motto of all the saints? Is that not also the ideal for all Christians? From the moment when God became the absolute, no human love could be absolute (Mk 10:22–31), no creature, no institution, no homeland, no earthly ideal....I can give of myself passionately to my professional duties, socially or politically. I can be a militant, totally devoted to transforming society into a more just and fraternal one. I can dedicate my life to help the most needy. I can be deeply attached to my own congregation and its founder. These are all legitimate and good, especially if I perform them with love, but nothing in all of this constitutes an absolute. Only God is great.

O my God, only you are God. By taking a step back in silent adoration, I want to situate and judge everything in this divine light: my work, my family, my activities, all that which is dear to my heart. Where is my treasure?

It is true that the more I love you, O my God, the more my heart grows larger and the more I will love. Let us vow with Brother Charles: "No longer God alone, but God first, and all of his creatures for him—because he loves them, because he

orders that they be loved, because they are his creatures, because they are a reflection of him....In the same way as we
love the children of a woman we love" (LLM, 96).

REFLECTION QUESTIONS

How do you experience the presence of God in your life? Do
you quiet yourself, letting go of anxiety and fear and allowing
God to fill you with his presence? Have you allowed faith to
open your heart to the experiences of God that surround you?

things to you so that my joy may be in you, and that your joy may be complete" (Jn 15:9–11).

Lord, you were so close to your final agony and you spoke to us of joy! How could you be happy at the time of your crucifixion? Are the cross and joy compatible?

Superimposed on your face, I see the face of my friend Joseph, sitting on his bed, a basin on his knees where his bloody sputum is accumulating. Instinctively, I tied this together with your bloody perspiration. At a time when we are plunged into anguish, my friend, between two spits of blood, smiles, and jokes. Even as he chokes and struggles for breath or suffers from sadness, his florid face is transfigured. At that moment, the light from his eyes reflects the joy of his Lord.

This vision causes me to think on the times when I am haunted by a mass of preoccupations or when I am hurt by a recent dispute, when I am ill or discouraged. How, in these times, can I rejoice in a happiness that I do not feel? How can I have a share of your joy, Lord?

I must humbly learn to forget myself and "decenter" my thoughts and interior ramblings "because it is you I love and, through you, I establish my egoism"; because it is you I am seeing, "I only have to look at you while repeating to myself that you are happy" (QPR, 112). Let us consider this curious idea: that of establishing "through you, my egoism." Now, isn't that something only lovers discover?

But I must admit, Lord, that faith is at a disadvantage. At a time when concrete worries and joys monopolize my feelings, my understanding, and my memory, it does not seem to be natural that the certainty of God's love for us and his infinite happiness would touch me in the same immediate way, with the same force. It is not easy to live what Brother Charles recommended to his sister: "When you suffer, think of the happiness of the Heart of Jesus; say to yourself that it is his happiness you want and not your own. His, the one you love, not your own. And amidst your ills, sadness, worries, troubles, and trials, rejoice in his infinite, unchanging happiness and in his immense peace" (ES, 226–227).

Lord, to what lengths are you calling me to reach this level of imperviousness, this disinterest in my spiritual attitude! At the price of what kind of personal sacrifice is this achieved? How can I attain a sense of joy in a happiness that I know, but do not feel, and to rejoice in this happiness without even hoping to feel it? As Brother Charles says: "Love consists not in feeling love but in wanting to love" (LLM, 205). When I manage to forget myself in order to take care of you, Lord, and my brothers, you will give me the gift of your own joy, even if I had not sought it.

I agree, Lord, to rejoice in the happiness of God, without considering myself, even if it is difficult. But when I see my brothers suffer, when I hear the cries of the poor, the cries of the pain and injustice, should I close my eyes and block my ears?

Lord, I have learned the answer to this question through contemplation. You have told me and retold me: "If you know me, you will know my Father also" (Jn 14:7) and "Whoever has seen me, has seen the Father" (Jn 14:9). How do you react when faced with human suffering? Hundreds of times, the gospels repeat that you are "moved with compassion." Your disciples saw you in tears before Lazarus' tomb and overflowing with pity for the crowds who came to you. With what conviction did you proclaim for centuries: "Come to me, all you that are weary and carrying heavy burdens, and I will give you rest. Take my yoke upon you, and learn from me; for I am gentle and humble in heart, and you will find rest for your souls" (Mt 11:28–29).

Lord, you show me your heart and this heart manifests the heart of God. If he is infinitely happy, my God is not an impassive God. He doesn't take refuge in the midst of his bliss in an indifferent transcendence. The heart of God beats eternally in mankind's chest.

Lord Jesus, you were disturbed when you saw the distress of the widow of Nain, and you gave her dead son life. You gave him back to his mother (Lk 7:12–15). This marvelous gesture was not planned; it came from a surge of your heart, out of "pure compassion."

With that fervor I must "receive your lessons," the lessons of your heart. As if I was hearing this exhortation from your very mouth, through the pen of Brother Charles: "See how sympathetic I am for you, how I suffer, how I am sorry, and have compassion for all the pain, how I sigh with these, how I cry with others....I have compassion for their losses, their illnesses, their worries, their hunger, their weaknesses, their ignorance and, above all, their sins....My Heart has deep compassion for all of the ailments of the soul and of the body....Compassion is part of love in the mortal heart and in all human love. Since I ask you to love your brothers, be sympathetic to all their ailments, big and small, suffer with them through whatever is making them suffer....Never forget the duty of love which is compassion....Don't forget my tears and sighs and these miracles I performed without being asked, to raise the sons from the dead, returning them to their mothers. May each of you say, at the moment of your death: 'Who among you cried when I didn't cry with you?' Oh, the one who is able to say that will be blessed a thousand times" (CE 59–60). Lord Jesus, may your everlasting heart prolong your compassion so that it will shine through me onto those who surround me.

Human suffering stimulates my compassion. The vision of evil, poverty, and injustice drives me to apply myself to suppress them—Brother Charles fought against slavery—and this lucid action aligns itself well to a heart that is pure and peaceful. Indeed, where joy reigns "no one will take your joy from you" (Jn 16:22). Even knowing my sins and my mediocrity should not sadden me, since Brother Charles consoles me with these words: "We are worried when we are not saddened by seeing the excess of evil that reigns everywhere...and by seeing ourselves so miserable after so many blessings....And yet, we must not be sad, but look beyond what happens toward our Beloved, since it is he whom we love and not ourselves. (...) If he is happy, we are happy" (LMB, 163–164).

So that we know, in our hearts, this simultaneous suffering and joy, a disciple of Brother Charles invites us to consider these thoughts: "Christmas is a feast day of joy. This does not stop some of us from suffering. There is a great difference between sadness and pain. Sadness makes you withdraw into yourself, but we have the right to suffer, even on Christmas Day, while thinking about those who are spending this day in jail, being tortured, and so on. But there may also be joy in your heart all the same...." Little Sister of Jesus Magdeleine addressed her students in 1976, illustrating this reflection of Brother Charles: "The more we love, the more intense joy and pain will be. Both of them grow together" (LFT, 160).

O Jesus, let me always keep before my eyes the sight of your joyful and compassionate Heart! And then, as you predicted on the evening of Holy Thursday, speaking about pain and joy: "So you have pain now; but I will see you again, and your hearts will rejoice, and no one will take your joy from you. On that day, you will ask nothing of me" (Jn 16:22–23).

REFLECTION QUESTIONS

Am I willing to acknowledge my self-love? When sadness and discouragement come over me, do I turn to Jesus and seek his strength? Can I turn away from my own suffering and notice Jesus suffering in others? How do I desire the compassion of Jesus to manifest itself in me?

DAY THREE

Our Beloved Lord Jesus

FOCUS POINT

Through our baptism we are called to follow the gospel of Jesus, to live the gospel with our lives. Imitation of Jesus Christ in all our actions is the call of spirituality. By our lives lived in union with Jesus, we witness to the world that Christ is risen and living in our midst.

Jesus said, it was his first words to his apostles, his first words to those who thirsted to know him: "Venite et videte." Begin by "coming," by following me, by imitating me, by practicing my teachings and then you "will see;" you will enjoy the light, in the same measure as you will have practiced....Venite et vedite: Oh how I have seen the truth in these words through my experience (LHC, 100).

The Brothers and Sisters of the Sacred Heart of Jesus take as their rule to ask themselves, in all things, what Jesus would have thought, said, and done in their situation and to do that. They make a constant effort to make themselves more and more like Our Lord Jesus, using his life in Nazareth as a model, which provides examples for all things. Imitation is measured in love (RD, 614).

The Passion and Calvary were supreme declarations of love. Jesus, you did not suffer so much just to redeem us!...The least of your acts carries an infinite price since it was an act of God and it would have been overabundantly sufficient to redeem a thousand worlds....It was to bring us, draw us, to freely love you because love is the most powerful way to attract love, because to love is the most powerful way to be loved.... (...) Since he has made his declaration of love in this way to us, let us imitate him by giving him our own declaration of love....It is not possible for us to love without imitating him, to love him without wanting to be what he was, to do what he did, to suffer and die in torment, it is not possible for us to love and want to be crowned with roses when he was with thorns (MSE, 250).

Y ou are reunited with the disciples for the Passover meal. Faced with stunned glances and Peter's reprobation, you came, Lord Jesus, to silently wash the feet of your apostles. When, having resumed your place at the table, you explained to them what you had just done, you were also addressing us: "Do you know what I have done to you? You call me Teacher and Lord—and you are right, for that is what I am.

So if I, your Lord and Teacher, have washed your feet, you also ought to wash one another's feet. For I have set you an example, that you should also do as I have done to you. Very truly, I tell you, servants are not greater than their master…" (Jn 13:12–16). These last words reminded his followers of a similar maxim that Jesus had told them at the beginning of their life with him: "A disciple is not above the teacher, but everyone who is fully qualified will be like the teacher" (Lk 6:40).

O Lord, it was like this in the beginning and at the end of your public life. You call us to imitate you, to be your disciple. To be a Christian is to want to imitate you. This recommendation applies to everyone, from the highest of the bishops to the most anonymous of the faithful.

O Jesus, your disciple, in effect, has nothing in common with the follower who is devoted to some historical figure. No, Lord, you are yet alive, and each of us has a personal relationship with you. After your Resurrection, when you reinstated Peter, who had denied knowing you, as the head of the apostles, you did not reproach him in any way. You did not ask if he agreed with a doctrine or a program. You did not question him about his abilities. You asked him this single question: "Do you love me?" (Jn 21:15ff.).

By contemplating this scene, I hear your words echo all the way to me. And I want to throw myself at your feet and say to you, with all my heart: "Yes, Lord Jesus, you know it; I do love you." I want to love you with a love that cannot be expressed in words, but which draws me to follow in your footsteps each and every day, because you have no use for those who are just satisfied to say "Lord, Lord." Brother Charles wrote: "Love cannot be separated from imitation. Whoever loves wants to imitate: it is the secret of my life. Nineteen hundred years ago I gave my heart to the crucified Jesus of Nazareth, and I live my life seeking to imitate him" (LGT, 159).

Lord, up to what point should I imitate you? What do you expect of me? I know that "imitation is measured in love." Make arrangements so that I may love you with all my heart, for "resemblance to the Beloved is a violent need of the heart" (OS, 602). Sincerely, I dare not, as Brother Charles had the habit of doing, call you "my Beloved," in the event that there is a gap, which I deplore, between the thrust of my word and my true feelings. Your loving friendship toward us, to the contrary, only knows fullness and faithfulness. Your cross is the "supreme declaration of love" that you give me every day. And each Mass repeats to me, with thunderous impact: "I loved you before your birth. I have taught you that there is no greater proof of love than to give one's life for those we love. I gave you this proof. I give it to you, my chosen friend. Here is my body, here is my blood that I shed for you, for all." Are not these words too often masked by the noise of my life? Do I forget that the Eucharist is a rendezvous of love?

In order to resemble you, it is not necessary to copy you. That would be impossible: I am not a carpenter and I don't live in Palestine; I travel by subway and not by donkey (see CE, 30). To be able to know what you would say and what you would do in my place, I must be so filled with your spirit that it almost spontaneously bursts out. It is not necessary to adhere to a program or to respectfully follow a rule, but to be another You, similar yet different. At times, I dream of being "the monstrance," about which Father Huvelin spoke to Brother Charles: "to show Jesus," there, where I live. "I would like to be good enough so that someone says: if the servant is such, then how must the master be?" (CT, 189).

To fill myself with your spirit, I only know the way taught by Brother Charles: to contemplate you, to listen to you, each day, by reading the gospel. Brother Charles admonishes: "Find the time to read a few lines of the Holy Gospel. (...) We fill ourselves with the spirit of Jesus by reading and rereading, by meditating and remeditating continuously upon his teachings and his examples; so that they are like a drop of water that falls and falls again in our souls, always at the same place" (LLM, 166–167). Do all things because it is "according to the Gospel of Jesus, according to the teachings of Jesus, the examples of Jesus, the advice of Jesus, the teachings of Jesus" that we will be judged (MSE, 478).

Lord Jesus, since you invite me, these days, to join myself to the prayers of Brother Charles, I would like to spend the time, as he did, "keeping company" with you. He said: "Why do I want to enter the religious life? To keep company with Our Lord as much as possible during his sorrows" (LMB, 22). Later, in the midst of this intimacy, he will seize the full amplitude of a perfect communion with you and he will not be able to keep company with you without uniting himself with your will to be the savior. And that passion will draw him, not only to pray and make penance for the salvation of humankind, but to take himself "out to the people," among "the most abandoned souls, the ones who have been left out the most."

What a high calling it is to keep company with you, Jesus. But what rank do you really take in my life? Are you first among those I love the most in this world? How much time do I spend with you each week? Each day? How do I pass this time? There are a hundred possible ways. To begin with, in the moments of silent prayer where I do nothing other than be with you, where I "lose time," freely, in your honor; where I repeat to you that I admire you, that I want to be your friend, your little brother; where I expect nothing more than to please you, "in a pure loss of my self, for you alone" (MSE, 428).

At other times, by contemplating a scene from the gospel, I try to push myself forward, in thought, through the crowds of people who are described there. I passionately listen to what you say to your listeners; or else, as I draw closer to you, I make the effort to share what you feel, to vibrate in unison in your joy and anger, to accompany you, day after day, hour after hour, through the last weeks of your life on earth, to get myself invited to Bethany, to suffer with you at the foot of the cross. But in these meditations, I look for no personal gain, no sense of personal accomplishment. As Brother Charles tells us: "I want to do them not for me, not for anyone, but I want them to be done solely to glorify you, to console you as much as possible" (QPR, 107). Each meditation that I dedicate to your Sacred Heart is like a rose that I place on the altar of my chapel.

Certainly, some days, I am overrun with work. I don't have a single minute for myself, and I don't have a single minute for you. Did you not experience this same thing in your public life, the days of great disturbance, when you and the apostles did not even have time to eat, when your family felt that you had lost your mind? Nevertheless, you knew to withdraw from the action and spend hours praying to your Father: "In the morning, while it was still very dark, he got up and went out to a deserted place, and there he prayed" (Mk 1:35). And, for myself, is it really certain that the other day I didn't have a minute? Do I never waste time in front of the television? Can I not imitate you in solitary prayer? Is it so difficult to keep company with you when you talk with our Father? I pray, along with Brother Charles, that you "arrange it so that I do not lose a single moment of heart-to-heart conversations with

you" (MSE, 246). "Therefore, imitate Jesus through love, contemplate Jesus through love, act in all things through love for
Jesus..." (MSE, 264).

REFLECTION QUESTIONS

Do I desire intimacy with Jesus? Is the gospel familiar to me?
Do I spend time meditating on the gospels? Do I acknowledge
that through baptism I am called to follow Jesus by living my
life in witness to the gospel?

DAY FOUR

Poor With Jesus

FOCUS POINT

The gospels present to us Jesus who through his poverty preaches the message of love. Jesus came to us as a servant. His ministry of preaching, healing, and reconciliation calls us to imitate him in offering healing and mercy to others. No matter what our position on the social ladder of life we are called to poverty of spirit, to live simply and generously for others.

My Lord Jesus, how quickly the ones who love you with all their heart will be poor; for they couldn't suffer being richer than their Beloved. How quickly the ones who think that what they do to one of your children they also do to you will be poor. How quickly the ones who think that all that is not done for them is not done for you. How quickly will this way of thinking permeate all the problems that are encountered. How quickly will the ones who receive your words with true faith be poor.

For you have said, if you want to be perfect, sell all that you have and give it to the poor, and blessed are the poor.

My God, I don't know if it is possible for certain souls to see you poor and to voluntarily remain rich, to see themselves greater than their master, than their Beloved, and not to want to resemble you as much as they can, in your humbling circumstances. I want all these people to love you, my God, but yet I believe that they are missing something in their love. In any event, I cannot conceive of love without a need, an urgent need to conform, to resemble the one who is loved. To be rich when you, my Lord, had been poor and living only by hard work does not seem to be a mark of love. For myself, my God...I cannot love in this way...(DP, 174–175).

The Brothers and Sisters of the Sacred Heart must remember that in order to be united with the Sacred Heart of Jesus, one must have the same desires as Jesus has. He did not damn the rich, but he did not praise wealth. He praised poverty....What, after all, did he choose for himself? (...) The Brothers and Sisters must weigh the value of God's advice and his example. They pray and reflect in order to know God's special will for them in those situations which concern wealth and poverty....They will always have the One Unique Model before them: the carpenter, the son of Mary (RD, 621, 622).

This young person who came to you, Lord, immediately pleased you by the righteousness of his behavior and the sincerity of his search. He asked, "Good Teacher, what must I do to inherit eternal life?" And it was out of goodness that you gave him the advice: "There is still one thing lacking. Sell all that you own and distribute the money to the poor, and you will have treasure in heaven: then come, follow me" (Lk 18:22). Seeing him depart in sadness, you exclaimed to the apostles: "How hard it is for those who have wealth to enter the king-dom of God!" (Lk 18:24).

For Brother Charles, Jesus was so alive to him in the present that time telescoped. In his prayers, Brother Charles acted as if he lived contemporaneously with Jesus and his life on earth. He thought of Jesus as a baby in the manger in Bethlehem and accompanied him in his flight to Egypt. "Then," he declared, "we will wait thirty years and will go to the desert for forty days" (LFT, 171). Brother Charles looked at Jesus as if he were a companion to Jesus as he leaned over the workbench in Nazareth, as he made his living by the sweat of his brow, as he then lived by the donation of alms. Charles saw him, in the present, stripped of everything on the Cross...and he felt car-ried to share his poverty with him, "all worries, difficulties, harshness, and difficult times of life...all the crosses."

Is not the amazing example of the humility of the One "who came to live amidst man, like one of them," enough to make us learn to minimize the allure of human greatness and the prestige of wealth? "From the time of his birth, he continues to teach us by his own example and to preach pov-erty, abjection, and suffering...." Later, "he appeared to be like a lowly worker...[and so I must] become as small as my master in order to be with him, step for step, to walk behind him, as a faithful servant, a faithful disciple...a faithful brother" (DP, 52, 53).

We could truly describe the entire life of Jesus as a descent: "He did nothing but descend: he descended to the Incarna-tion, by making himself a small child, by obeying; he descended by making himself...poor, forsaken, exiled, persecuted, executed, by always putting himself in last place" (VN, 208).

Here I am, Lord Jesus, living in the twentieth century and, at the same time, following in your footsteps by imitating your poverty. And if I hear your exhortations to live in poverty, to choose between God and money, to sell all my worldly goods and to give the proceeds to the poor, I must admit that I will be upset by it. We are not all going to be monks and religious.

What is God's will for us, for me, regarding poverty? Lord Jesus, you who knew family life, you who lived "in the midst of the world," enlighten me, make it so that I have a generous nature, and, if it seems to be necessary, to question the way that I live. Even if I must be prudent and protect myself with many precautions, make it so that I do not forget to abandon myself to divine Providence and that this trust, even if it is a little foolish, will not be completely lost in the midst of my calculations.

No matter what kind of concrete expression of poverty I am called to follow, one thing is certain: if I love my brothers and sisters, I could not be wealthy. If I am concerned for any needy person who knocks at my door, then it is to the Lord himself that I must open it. And even if he is not nearby, if he is at the other end of the world, dying of hunger or leprosy, this needy person is still my brother. "When we love our neighbor, the first fruit of this love is to accept even poverty in order to soothe him....Poverty, love of our neighbor: we see how these two virtues are closely tied together" (PFJ, 88).

Since we have received without payment, we should give without payment (Mt 10:8); and this is done "by putting all the riches of our body and soul at the disposal of our neighbor, all that we have and all that we are" (PFJ, 34). We are only the managers of our material goods. "We should consider ourselves as servants, as people charged with the job of taking care of a deposit that our master has entrusted to us" (RD, 623).

Lord Jesus, I cannot run away from your demands. Even if I turn my face away from you, even if I close the book of the gospel and put it away, you come back in the guise of one of my brothers. I find you always along my route. I want to be generous, but what you are asking of me is difficult. Perhaps if I loved you more it would seem easier.

When the Father General authorized Brother Charles to leave the Trappists, he uttered his private vows, in particular, the one of "perpetual poverty" by which he promised "never to have in his possession or for his use more than a poor laborer could own" (VN, 28). It is in this promise that we find the seed of a new idea which upset religious life: the passing from legal to social poverty. We continue, certainly, to renounce all rights to property but, even more, we commit ourselves to "live the life of the poor" (MSE, 199). This is the same program as that proposed by Brother Charles, some months later, in his meditations: "Like Jesus, be poor, which consists of living like the poor, having no place to live, nothing to eat, no clothing or personal effects other than the basics that poor people have. Do not live in conventional poverty, but the poverty of the poor" (MSE, 285). All of the religious who consider Brother Charles to be their father, all who espouse his plentiful spiritual legacy, strive, as situations dictate, to make this prophetic in-spiration concrete.

Emulating the poor of our times does not separate you or me from our prayer and, certainly, separates us even less from you, Lord Jesus, who lived among the poor. The children and the poor, those to whom we too often attach little importance, were your favorites, O Lord. The type of poverty which Brother Charles claimed for his brothers and sisters—and which he embraced until his death—was one that permitted the poor to find themselves in a fraternity at the same level.

Our vocations are diverse—and we should judge no one on this score—but we are all called to the beatitude of being one with "those who have the soul of a poor person" and to the freedom of those who have renounced everything (Lk 14:33). "To renounce everything in spirit, to be detached from everything of the heart, to be poor in spirit, emptied of all attachments, is absolutely indispensable to become a disciple of Jesus" (PFJ, 92).

Do I doubt the authenticity of my poverty of heart and feel that it is just an illusion? But, think, if poor, downtrodden, suffering, voiceless, marginalized, and unhappy people feel at ease with me, just as they felt at ease with Jesus, I will have my proof of authenticity.

"In everything, we must never stop being poor, the brothers of the poor, friends of the poor" (MSE, 263) in order to be "on your side," Lord Jesus. Help me make Brother Charles's sentiments my own, when he put all of his heart in this prayer of poverty, which he uttered in a hut in Nazareth—a prayer that begins by speaking of love: "My Lord Jesus, how quickly the one who loves you with all his heart will be poor, for they could not suffer being richer than their Beloved."

REFLECTION QUESTIONS

What feelings well up within you about poverty? Do you see poverty as a way of imitation of Christ? Are there ways you can simplify your life? What are two ways you can live poverty of spirit?

DAY FIVE
Let Jesus Live Within

FOCUS POINT

In the Eucharist we encounter the living Jesus. He is present in us and continues his life in us by our imitation of his virtues. The gospel comes alive in us and those around us when we live by the teachings of Jesus found in them. We allow the mystery of Christ to flower in us through deeds of love and mercy toward others.

You dwell in a faithful soul, my Lord, entering into it and making your dwelling there. You become like a soul for the soul; your grace supports it, leads it, enlightens its intelligence, and steers its will in everything. It no longer acts on its own, it is you who acts in it....You give it life, a life of grace, the seed of a life of glory, with a growing abundance. (...) Jesus, by living in a faithful soul, you use it to glorify God and to sanctify humans, thus prolonging its mortal life and making a second Himself (DP, 88–89).

Our Lord asks us to let the life continue in us that he began on earth in the womb of the Blessed Virgin. (...) Let him live in us, let his hidden life in Nazareth continue in us, let his life of poverty continue in us, let his life of universal charity continue in us, let his life of humility be prolonged in us. Let us, through our faithfulness in practicing penance, achieve in us what was missing in his suffering. Let Jesus, by our zeal for souls, continue to light a fire on earth. Let him, by our vigils and prayers, continue, in us, to spend entire nights in prayer to God. (...) By making each moment of our lives become moments of his life, all our thoughts, our words, and actions become thoughts, words, and actions that are no longer natural or human, but divine, no longer our own, but those of Jesus. Let us have the power to say, at each moment of our existence: "I live, but it is not I who live, it is Jesus who lives within me" (ED, 303–304).

Lord Jesus, your betrayal and death is approaching, and you do not want to abandon us. You have just bequeathed this memorial mystery which is the Eucharist to us at the Last Supper. Furthermore, you have announced: "Those who love me will keep my word, and my Father will love them, and we will come to them and make our home with them" (Jn 14:23).

Do we realize the unbelievable meaning of this simple sentence? We are the dwellings of a living God. Or, as the first Christians termed it, we are to become Christ-bearers, Christ-carriers, since we live off his life which springs from his presence within us. This truth, which the Fathers of the Church sum up in the phrase "God made himself become man so that man will become God" can make our heads spin. During each Mass, the priest reminds us of this truth by pouring a few drops of water into the chalice; just as the water mixes with the wine may we be united with the divinity of the one who assumed our humanity. We are deified. That is the big news which, each day, dims the news we receive on television or in the newspapers.

Lord Jesus, I need not search outside of myself for you. You are within me, not like a bauble in a jewel box, but like a wellspring of life, like the sap which irrigates and replenishes the vine, all the way down to the smallest stems (Jn 15:5–6). When I speak of imitation, my goal is not to reproduce a model of the exterior, but the interior, in just the same way as a sprout comes forth from a divine vine—an offspring through which the Lord's teachings are fulfilled and his image and acts extended. Through the offspring, the Lord continues and prolongs his life, which was actually limited to only thirty-three years, but through all those that the Lord deifies, his life crosses time and space. Then, all these human actions will, at the same time, become divine, whether they are the most genial or the most ordinary. Whether it is harvesting potatoes or chanting the liturgical offices, it is the Lord Jesus who assumes these activities through us, just as he does with our daily joys and sorrows. Even in our cars, the Lord never leaves us: and his presence behind the wheel can change our way of driving! This astounding deification of each of us is realized in the diversity of our characters and the immense range of human cultures. The Lord makes as his own the life of a mother or the works of an astronaut, the labors of a peasant or calculations of an engineer, the essence of a pygmy or of a Mongolian, a Dene, or a Maori.

A disciple of Brother Charles, Albert Peyriguère, taught us by saying: "Christ lives in you....He doesn't leave you for a single instant and, consequently, you do not leave him for a single instant. No matter what you do, he is there within you; he is you. There is no distinction to be made between the moments when you are with Christ in prayer or the moments when you are less to him. You are continuously in him and he in you."

O Lord, may this divine life within me never be snuffed out through my own fault. It is a life that tends to grow and blossom. Yes, in spite of my weaknesses or my mediocrities, you live in me: As Brother Charles contemplates: "I remain a sinner...and that is one of the things that has, for a long time, contributed to preventing me from looking for you in myself so that I can adore you....I was frightened to feel you so deep within me, so close to my miseries, so aware of my countless imperfections. (...) Forgive me, help me....I am yours, my body, my soul, all that I am is yours: It is no longer I who live, but you who live within me, O Jesus. Continue your life in me...for the greater glory of God. Amen. And grant this same grace to all people so that you will be glorified by all people. Amen" (CFA, 526, 528).

Lord Jesus, through me, you want to love all the human beings that you put on my route. To my love for them your love adds "strength, stability, devotion, an ardor that purely human love does not have" (RD, 634). When I love like you, your heart and mine beat in the same rhythm. It is you yourself and it is your heart that moves my own and loves through me with a "universal charity" toward all my brothers, all your brothers (see LLM, 96).

Through my hospitality, my smile, as well as through the charitable actions that I perform, your divine tenderness reaches out to our brothers and sisters in an anonymous way, for they do not know that through me it is unquestionably you who loves them.

O Jesus, for the sick person who suffers, you turn their suffering into your own: through that person, you complete "what is lacking in your own sufferings" (Col 1:24) and you redeem the world in this sick and suffering person by your filial "yes" which is perpetuated in that sick person's own "yes." Suffering "is not good in itself," for did you not, O Jesus, spend a great deal of time curing the sick during your public life? But what counts is the "here I am," and the "See, I have come to do your will" (Heb 10:9) (see MSE, 163).

So that our hearts pray as much as our lips, Brother Charles recommends that we keep ourselves lovingly at God's feet, in order to contemplate him, to admire him, to desire his glory and consolation, and, in a single phrase, express "all those feelings that inspire love" (EJ, 26). When I remind myself of this charge and of the true definition of love, I come to hate the mediocrity of my prayers and I am tempted to be discouraged. But the conviction that it is not I who is praying but you prevents me from this despair. It is you, Lord Jesus, who prays in me and through me. May your presence give an infinite range to my poor prayer. If I am unable to give thanks as I should, I say to you: "Lord, thank yourself in me; make in me recognition, thanksgiving, faith, love…" (DP, 109).

This prayer from Jesus, by incarnating on earth like a seed, grows to universal dimensions and is expressed in a multitude of languages and cultures. It assumes the work, desires, sorrows, and sentiments that Jesus could not have known at the time of his earthly existence. Through its mystical prolongation, the Incarnation is unfurled and enriched immensely.

Brother Charles, through his meditations and letters, endlessly repeated, like a sublime refrain, what the apostle Paul confided in Galatians 2:20: "It is no longer I who live, it is Christ who lives in me. And the life I now live in the flesh I live by faith in the Son of God, who loved me and gave himself for me." In the same way, Brother Charles repeated this to a correspondent numerous times: "May Jesus guide you, enlighten you, may he live more and more in you, so that more and more it is no longer you who lives, but Him living in you" (LLM, 84).

REFLECTION QUESTIONS

Brother Charles presents to us a very detailed spirituality of the mystery of Jesus living in us. What thoughts come to mind when you read the comments of Brother Charles on the hidden life of Jesus continuing in each of us? How do you experience God living in you? Do you desire to be transformed into the presence of Jesus through a life of service and simplicity directed toward the poor and neglected of our society?

DAY SIX

Proclaim the Gospel by the Way We Live

FOCUS POINT

Often we except ourselves from the task of preaching the gospel. We leave that to those who feel called to ministry in the Church. Brother Charles understands the call of the gospel as radical union with Christ. We are to witness by our lives lived in the spirituality of the gospels. We preach the kingdom of God by our thoughts, words, and deeds done with love.

Jesus speaks these words to me: Even before I was born I was working on this mission, the sanctification of man...and I urged my mother to work at it with me. (...) One day I will say to my apostles: preach, and I will give them their mission. Here, I say to other souls, to all of those who have me within them but have not received their mission to preach, I tell them to sanctify souls simply by carrying me within themselves in silence. (...) Everyone, work toward the sanctification of the world, work at it as my mother does; silently, without words, go and establish your prayerful retreats in the midst of those who ignore me. And carry the Gospel with you, not by preaching it with your mouths, but by preaching it through your examples, not by proclaiming it, but by living it. Sanctify the world, take me into the world...as Mary took me to John (CE, 21, 22).

We do good, not by what we say and do, but by what we are, by the grace which accompanies our actions, by the way that Jesus lives within us, by the way that our actions are Jesus' actions, working in and through us....The soul does good works by its holiness. May we always see this truth (RD, 645–646).

Our entire existence and being should shout the Gospel from the rooftops. Our entire person should breathe Jesus. All our actions and our entire life should proclaim that we belong to Jesus. Our lives should be a mirror image of an evangelical life. Our entire being should be a living sermon, a reflection of Jesus, a scent of Jesus, something that proclaims Jesus, that makes others see Jesus and that shines like an image of Jesus (MSE, 314).

I n a few seconds, Lord Jesus, you will definitively disappear from the eyes of the apostles. What advice are you going to give them at this supreme instant? What are your last words here on earth? Are these words not addressed to us as well: "But you will receive power when the Holy Spirit has come upon you; and you will be my witnesses in Jerusalem, in all Judea and Samaria, and to the ends of the earth" (Acts 1:8)?

Lord, to be your witness, is it not by being your image, by being a "living gospel"? Father Charles says: "People who are far from Jesus should, without books or words, be able to know the Gospel by seeing my life....By seeing me, they should see what is Jesus" (RD, 647). What a responsibility! It takes nothing less than the holiness of the witness to accomplish. Do we rely upon a person's speeches when the life of the orator does not reflect his words? Father Peyriguère has remarked: "Perhaps living Christ is the supreme way to speak of him. There are too many apostles to speak about him and not enough to live him."

In order to get to the heart of things, the requirement is, above all, one of transparency. Lord Jesus, if it is you who lives in me, may it be your words that come from my mouth and your actions that I fulfill, for says Father Peyriguère: "All the mystery of the apostolate resides in taking things from within." If it is you who lives in me, it is you who acts beyond my actions and gives them their true effectiveness. If I ignore what happens—invisibly—in my relationships with others, if the "results" of these friendships cannot be compatible with the apostolic statement, indeed, Lord, you know. Why do I need to know?

Lord, make it so that I do not seek my own success, but that it is you who acts through me. Make it so that my witness will be selfless because, says Varillon, "the will of the witness destroys the witness." Make it so that I am a docile instrument in your hands. Every instrument is different from another: each keeps its intelligence and personality, each has its gifts and limitations. For a work of art to come to fruition, it is not the paintbrush that counts, but the artist. Lord, you alone are the one who evangelizes. And may I not even realize that I am a witness.

Brother Charles offers Mary, in the mystery of the Visitation, as a model of this docility in evangelization. She evangelized and sanctified Saint John "not by her words but by silently carrying Jesus close to him, to his dwelling." Following her example, we should "evangelize and sanctify the unfaithful by carrying Jesus to their midst in silence, by carrying him, our evangelical life, in our own lives which should provide an example of his. We should be seen as living images of the Christ that we carry" (CFA, 472).

Brother Charles, by commenting on this part of the gospel (the Visitation story as told in Luke 1:39–41), tends to idealize the motives of the Blessed Virgin. In his writings, this very ordinary familial step takes on the allure of a procession of the Blessed Sacrament! Mary "carried Jesus inside herself," as we do after holy Communion, "with continuous meditation, contemplation, and adoration" (CFA, 473). According to Brother Charles, she did not go to visit her cousin "for mutual edification through the recitation of the marvels of God within her," and she did not even make the journey "for the purpose of a charitable visit to help her cousin in the last months of her pregnancy and in childbirth" (CFA, 472).

Why, I must ask myself, aren't these motives the ones uppermost in Mary's mind? Since the gospel points out that Mary visited her cousin for three months until the birth of Saint John the Baptist, I find myself thinking—and may Brother Charles pardon me for this—that it is very likely that Mary naturally wanted to confide in Elizabeth about the mystery which inhabited her and, very simply, wanted to give Elizabeth a helping hand. I find this admirable that she went to visit her cousin to help her in a spontaneous gesture of affection, without any forethought of taking Jesus to her. It would be through this type of ordinary thing that Jesus would have chosen to act.

Later, toward the end of his life, Brother Charles comments again on this wonderful feast. He wrote: "Charity doesn't do things halfway, but well and completely. The Most Blessed Virgin didn't visit Elizabeth for just a few days; she stayed there as long as it was necessary to do what she wanted" (EJ, 294).

For Brother Charles, this mystery of the Visitation symbolized the profound attitude which inspired the disciples' behavior with respect to human relationships. And in his visionary enthusiasm, when he was alone and did not have a single postulant, on July 2, 1904, he anticipated in his notebook the significant status of this feast in his mind by designating the feast day of the Visitation of the Most Blessed Virgin as the "patronal feast day for all the fraternities of Little Brothers and Little Sisters of the Sacred Heart of Jesus" (CB, 143).

Furthermore, Brother Charles did not envision only religious brothers and sisters as his spiritual posterity. The apostolate, the outreaching mission, was not, in his opinion, the sole privilege of specialists: lay people were also called to contribute. He wrote: "I know very well that God has called all Christians, men and women, religious and lay people, celibates and married people, to be apostles, apostles through their example, through kindness, through a beneficial contact." He continued, "All Christians should be apostles. This is not advice, it is a commandment. It is the commandment of charity" (LLM, 128, 271).

Strong in the conviction that Jesus, living within us, acts through us in all human relationships, we must go out to meet our brothers and sisters. Is respect not the first step on this road of fraternal love? With all feelings of superiority removed, you and I must want to deeply respect all human beings, cherish every way and every thing in which they are different from us, no matter what that difference may be. And we must want to love those persons entirely for themselves.

To a Muslim friend, who jokingly asked Brother Charles, "Are you praying for my conversion?" he replied: "No, I am not praying for your conversion; I am praying that you do the will of God." That statement says it all. I could hope for a change in my friend which would make me happy, but would that evolution correspond to the will of God? That is the ultimate test.

Lord Jesus, teach me this humble and patient respect for each person who accedes to "God's unknown plan" for him or her. Lord Jesus, teach me to freely love my brother in the same way as our Father's infinite tenderness loves each of us, freely. Lord Jesus, I believe that you want to act through me, arrange it so that I am transparent, deliver me from all opacity so that I can be a reflection of you, so that you can be seen through my life. Make it happen that I preach the gospel in silence each and every day. As Brother Charles prays: "My God, may your will be done in me and in all your creatures. My God, ensure that all humans go to heaven. Amen."

REFLECTION QUESTIONS

Do I consider myself as a preacher of the gospel? Have I thought about my actions being the only gospel some people ever read? Through prayer and reflection, do I allow Jesus to lead me to where he wants to be present?

DAY SEVEN
The Time for Nazareth Has Come

FOCUS POINT
There is very little written about the life of Jesus before his public ministry. We have a tradition of thirty years spent in a hidden life. It is this period of thirty years hidden in silence and work that Brother Charles takes as the centerpiece for his foundation of a new religious community.

God came to us to redeem us. He lived in our midst and had the closest contact possible from the time of the Annunciation to the Ascension. In order to redeem souls, he continues to be in our midst and live amongst us in the closest type of contact, each day and at all times in the Holy Eucharist. In this way, we should, in order to work for the salvation of souls, go to them, into their midst, live with them in the closest contact possible (RD, 649–650).

Take Jesus' life in Nazareth as an objective, in all things and for all things, in its simplicity and its greatness, by only using the Rule [of the Little Brothers] as a directory. Live just like Jesus of Nazareth—no special costume or habit, no cloister, no living apart from others, rather living close to them, no less than eight hours of work on a daily basis (preferably manual labor), no great land holdings, no large expenses, no acceptance of large gifts, but practice of extreme poverty in all things…in a short phrase, in all things, just like Jesus in Nazareth (CT, 46).

Jesus told us: "I spent my childhood years, my youth, and my adolescence in Nazareth….It was for your love that I led my life there as I did. (…) What did I teach you? I taught you to live off the work of your hands and not be reliant upon anyone and to have something to give to the poor. This type of life has an incomparable beauty that no other has if it is not a life of evangelical work, one which imitates mine….Those who live off the labors of their own hands and those that, while preaching the Gospel, live off the charity of others, imitate me…" (CE, 29–30).

L ord Jesus, when you came back to Nazareth with your disciples, the people who had known you were all astounded. How could an ordinary man, one whom they had seen grow and work in the same way as had the other youths in the village speak in this manner? "Where did this man get all this? What is this wisdom that has been given to him? What deeds of power are being done by his hands! Is not this the carpenter, the son of Mary?" (Mk 6:2–3).

For all time, you will always be Jesus of Nazareth, and, in Arabic countries in our time, your disciples are called "Nazaréens" (*Nesrani*). Brother Charles discovered that his vocation was to imitate you in your life in Nazareth in the manner and way, he notes pleasantly, as you lived at the time of your "election" and before your public life: "I am certainly not called to preach; my soul is not capable of it, not in the desert. My body can't live without food, therefore I am called to the life of Nazareth, a life which my body and soul can support and to which I am attracted" (SAD, 49).

Lord Jesus, your life in Nazareth was so ordinary that the gospel doesn't even give it two lines. All that we can affirm is that it was not the life of a hermit, but the life of a village craftsman. And, if we called it hidden, it was because you did not divulge your divine character, as you did in your public life, because you let nothing show on the surface about this mystery that dwelled within you. That mystery made you more than a carpenter who carried wood along the village roads. You passed for an ordinary man: and the villagers thought they knew everything about you. Later, not without annoyance, you would exclaim: "You know me, and you know where I am from. I have not come on my own. But the one who sent me is true, and you do not know him" (Jn 7:28).

Lord Jesus, how similar to us you are, just like a factory worker or an office worker, just like a person who has to work to earn a living, just like one who feels tired at the end of the day. You must have haggled over prices with a merchant or, at times, felt the uncertainty of an self-employed worker who had yet to receive an order. You had a relationship with your cousins, your neighbors, your friends. You shared the joys and sorrows of the residents of the village where everyone knew you. You participated in celebrations just like the marriage feast at Cana. You regularly went to the synagogue. How much your life is like our own! Brother Charles quotes you as telling us: "Your life in Nazareth can be lived everywhere. Live it closest to a place which is of the most use to your neighbors" (CT, 46–47).

Lord Jesus, by following in your footsteps and imitating you, we can live our daily lives a little like the one we might have lived if we were in Nazareth with you: "For each other, let us have thoughts, words, and actions that are suitable for that home in Nazareth, around the Blessed Virgin and Saint Joseph, and at the feet of Jesus..." (RD, 208).

Whether we are in the garden, the garage, or the kitchen, in front of the computer or the washing machine, swinging a hammer or a broom, let us take ourselves in spirit to Nazareth. "May the brother Sacristan do his job with faith, inner spirit, continuous contemplation, and with the love felt by the Blessed Virgin when she was sweeping her divine son's room, filling the lamps with oil, taking care of the laundry and the clothing, and wiping the furniture" (RD, 213).

Brother Charles insisted upon "the nobility and greatness of manual labor" (RD, 640), and he made this recommendation to the lay people of his Association: "Those among you whose work is mainly intellectual must include, in your day, some time spent in lowly and humble tasks, in order to grow through this imitation of the 'craftsman son of Mary,' to live something from the Holy Gospel in order to understand that Gospel. One does not understand something in the Gospel by hearing about it, but by doing it" (RD, 640).

"I came to bring fire to the earth and how I wish it were already kindled!" (Lk 12:49). Brother Charles made this ardent desire of Jesus his own: this phrase was possibly his favorite passage of the gospel. How passionately he aspired to "save" with Jesus! And he was ready to do anything for that: "You ask if I am willing to go somewhere other than Ben-Abbès to further the Holy Gospel? I am willing to do that and to go to the ends of the world and live until the time of the final judgment," he wrote (OS, 40).

Brother Charles made this desire his own, and found himself facing a world—a Muslim world—which, strong in its belief, considered all his attempts to proclaim the gospel as an intolerable attack against their faith. If any priests came to the Sahara to preach, "they were received like the Breton villages received the Turks who came to preach about Mahomet" (B, 407). Without a doubt, we would better appreciate this comparison if we took ourselves back to the situation in the Sahara in 1912, the year Brother Charles wrote these words.

Brother Charles learned to respect a religion other than his own and that led him to meditate on the mystery of God's plan. If "all direct evangelization is impossible," then what do we do? If it is not the time to preach, as Jesus did in his public life, we must conclude that it is time for a hidden life. And he placed, under the sign of Nazareth, all of his apostolic ardor, without diminishing it in the least. "I am not even sowing seeds: I am preparing the soil; others will plant the seeds, others will harvest, (...) God only knows when, perhaps in centuries" (LHC, 156, 182). Is not the situation of the Christian apostle in a secular world somewhat analogous?

Therefore, it is a time for witnessing, it is a time to "preach the Gospel in silence," just as did Jesus of Nazareth who was our Savior right from the very first moments of his earthly life. It is the time for human relationships, for friendships, just as it was for Jesus, who came to us in human form to redeem us, who lived in our midst in the closest possible contact with ordinary humans. O mysterious and admirable continuity, from the Incarnation to the Eucharist, and from the Eucharist which is taken in by each of us and all of those who surround us.

"Live amid" are the words that signify our mission. Lord Jesus, in each of us, you prolong your presence among our brothers, in the same way as you were there in Nazareth, sharing your work and ordinary life with your fellow villagers. You redeemed them in silence through your prayer, through your "spirit of sacrifice and penance." You spoke to them in silence by your life, your kindness, and your friendship.

Without any tactical motive, I offer my selfless friendship to those who are placed along my route by the Lord. According to the advice of Little Sister Magdeleine, who inspired her little community: "We should have the great desire to befriend all human beings, by going to them simply because we love them and we would like to give witness to them freely. That is to say, not expecting any recognition or result...or even an apostolate."

These communal bonds reverberate beyond the visible because it is friendship that is the language of the kingdom of God.

REFLECTION QUESTIONS

Do you experience your daily work and lifestyle as a means of witnessing the gospel? Throughout the day, do you pause and reflect on what you are doing and why? Do you pray often throughout the day through periods of silent recollection?

DAY EIGHT
The Word *Savior* Sums Up Our Life

―――

FOCUS POINT

The gospel calls us to imitate the compassionate love of Jesus in all our actions. We are to model ourselves on the Good Shepherd. We are to go in search of those who are left abandoned by society and the Church. We bring people to Christ by our love and kindness and our willingness to unite our sufferings to the sufferings of Jesus for the sake of the world.

―――

Jesus' name is so important in the eyes of God that he himself imposed it on Our Lord and made it known right from the time of his conception rather than leaving it to Mary and Joseph to name the divine child. This name, Jesus, therefore, is not human, but divine: it expresses a thought, a divine will. This thought is that Our Lord must be the savior of mankind:

45

so much so that this word "savior" is expressed with divine truth, exactitude, and divine perfection. What he is, that is what he did on earth. Jesus was incarnated in order to save the world, Jesus lived to save, think, speak, and act. Jesus saved us by dying on Calvary for us....

The extent of our membership in Jesus will be proportionate to our efforts as saviors of others: of all mankind, at each moment of our existence, so that each of our gestures, thoughts, words, and actions will be more useful to the salvation of all mankind (EJ, 147–148).

A single soul is worth more than the entire Holy Land, and more than all material creation combined. We must not go to a place where the land is the holiest but to a place where the souls are in the greatest of need....We must go where Jesus would go: to the lamb who has strayed the furthest, to Jesus' brother who is the most ill, to the most downtrodden...to those who are the most lost (SAD, 80, 83).

The main characteristics of the Little Brothers of the Sacred Heart are, first, to continuously imitate Our Lord Jesus in order to be his faithful images; and, second, to be zealots for souls: to fulfill the requirement to see a soul to save in all humans and to devote themselves to the salvation of souls as did their Beloved to the point that the name "savior" sums up their lives as it explains his (RD, 103, 104).

I n order to make it understood that "the Son of Man came to save that which was lost," Lord Jesus, you used a comparison which could do nothing but touch your listeners: "If a shepherd has a hundred sheep, and one of them has gone astray, does he not leave the ninety-nine on the mountains and go in search of the one that went astray? And if he finds it, truly I tell you, he rejoices over it more than over the ninety-nine that never went astray. So it is not the will of your Father in heaven that one of these little ones should be lost" (Mt 18:12–14).

How simple your words in the gospel are! No abstractions are used. In a familiar tone, you propose to impress truths and requirements on us which no one could miss. And, when the latter are gathered to the passionate heart of Brother Charles, and he comments on them, they seem to become a little frightening to us.

Brother Charles has retained Father Huvelin's maxim: "There can be excesses in all things except love" (CFA, 177). When we hear this and other of his instructions, and take them literally, we are tempted to consider them as impossible to put into practice—either by ourselves or by future disciples. Let us observe, meanwhile, that even in his own case, Brother Charles gives proof of flexibility in the application of his many resolutions from Nazareth. He says: "It is not necessary that the desire to offer the most sacrifices to God makes me live in a state of restraint and sadness...rather, to have the holy freedom of the children of God and be in God's joy is what is essential" (DP, 226). He also said: "A rule, yes, but also holy freedom in its application, as Jesus would do it..." (VN, 33). Later, in the Sahara, when he invoked the details of his Rule, to which he was so greatly attached, did he not agree to use it as a "directory," that is to say, as a defining spirit rather than a law which was meticulously construed to be totally constraining? The witnesses recognize and agree that, in his life, Brother Charles acted in a more "human" way than he indicated in his writings.

Do not be discouraged by the seemingly excessive and unwavering character of certain affirmations and axioms of Brother Charles. All the better if they disturb us and provoke a new spark. May our spirits drink up the sap of his meditations. May the breath which enlivens them nourish an ardent prayer and evangelical behavior in us. May we be seized by Brother Charles's contagious love for our beloved Jesus.

When Brother Charles asks us to see "a soul to save" in each human being, that does not mean that we must immediately take action, more or less indiscriminately to work for their conversion. Let us not forget that life in Nazareth at the time that Jesus lived there was characterized by respect and not by rashness. See even Brother Charles's reluctance to become a missionary rather than an exemplar when, in 1908, he wrote to his bishop: "Preach the Gospel to the Tuaregs? I don't believe that Jesus would have wanted it, not from me, not from anyone."

A soul to save: shouldn't the first one be our own? If we speak of conversion, is that conversion not first referring to us? So think of this conundrum: we are all already saved by Jesus and, at the same time, we are in the process of saving ourselves. Saint Paul invites us and all our human brothers and sisters to believe that we are made alive together with Christ and raised up and seated with him in the heavenly places (Eph 2:5–6).

We are charged to include all mankind in our prayer. Says Brother Charles, "Let us pray with the simplicity of Jesus, with his insistence, with his love for God and mankind....Let us pray a great deal for all mankind, since everyone is in Jesus' heart" (EJ, 108). As Brother Charles's follower, Father Peyriguère comments: To see all mankind as being "in Jesus' heart," isn't that just another way of saying that "all mankind is Christlike"?

A prayer such as the one above is the first of Brother Charles's listed ways for us to make a contribution to the salvation of humanity. And let us not hesitate "to ask God even the most difficult things, such as the conversion of great sinners and entire populations....Let us boldly ask for the things that are the most impossible to obtain...with the faith that God passionately loves us. The greater the gift, the more the one who loves passionately will love to give it" (EJ, 44).

Brother Charles's imitation of the Lord Jesus, which perhaps seems a personal matter between him and the Beloved, also becomes one of the suggested ways to save the world. This imitation of the Lord is one of the signs that indicate how far Brother Charles's evolution has come. His follower Peyriguère explains how, starting with the triad of "love, imitate, and console or keep company with," Father de Foucauld arrives at the fundamental equation "love Christ, imitate him, and be a savior like him" that sums up everything about him: his most profound mysticism and indeed his entire story.

Brother Charles believes that the more he converted and sanctified himself, the more he would be united with Christ in the process of saving the world. He writes: "The Holy Spirit brings one (...) to the pure and simple imitation of Jesus, as the best way to save souls" (CB, 70). This is indeed the invisible "apostolic efficiency of holiness."

Another way to allow Jesus to be a savior in us is through the spirit of sacrifice. "It is by the Cross that Jesus saved the world," says Brother Charles. "It is by the Cross, by letting Jesus live within us and achieve in us, it is by our sufferings that what was lacking in his Passion is achieved. It is by the Cross that we must continue, until the end of time, the work of the Redemption" (RD, 646). Did not Thérèse of Lisieux, in just this way, become the patroness of missions without ever leaving her Carmel? Charles and Thérèse are truly brother and sister—one by treading the paths of the desert and the other "by walking in the footsteps of a missionary" behind the gates of a Norman convent.

The spirit of sacrifice does not imply a systematic search for mortifications and austerities or extraordinary deprivations. Each moment of our daily lives, no matter how insignificant, makes up the warp and woof of our offering. "For an action to be a sacrifice, it must not have arisen from a need, because then it could have been offered before. Seeing that all actions, words, and good thoughts for which we take time can be offered to God as a sacrifice, it is not necessary to make a whole host of them, or think about them all day, or to say to ourselves 'let us make a sacrifice' all the time. It is enough to offer our thoughts, words, daily actions, movements, and our being to God each morning..." (DP, 226–227).

Lord Jesus, in thought, I kneel next to Thérèse of Lisieux and to Brother Charles. I join them by offering myself totally to you so that you continue to save the world through me. I pray: "My God, make it so that all mankind goes to heaven! Amen."

REFLECTION QUESTIONS

How have you experienced conversion in your life? How conscious are you of Christ's presence within you? Do you see the suffering in your life as an invitation from Jesus to allow him to manifest himself within you?

DAY NINE

The Universal Brother

FOCUS POINT

We are called to universal Christian fellowship, to see others as our brothers and sisters in Christ. This includes all types of persons, the outcast, the poor, even the most abject and ignorant of society. All humankind are children of God. Charles de Foucauld, by his life and example, has given us a prime example of inclusivity.

I would like to get all people, Christians, Muslims, Jews, and idolaters to see me as their brother, the universal brother. The people began to call my house "the Fraternity," and that touched me (OS, 39).

We are all the sons of the Most High. All of us: the poorest, the most outcast, a newborn child, a decrepit old man, the least intelligent human being, the most abject, an idiot, a fool, a sometimes sinner, the greatest sinner, the most ignorant, the last of the last, he who is the most physically and morally repugnant—all are children of God and sons and daughters of the Most High.

We should hold all human beings in high esteem. We should love all humankind, for they are children of God. God wants his children to love each other in the same way as a loving father wants his sons to love each other. Let us love all human beings because they are our brothers and sisters, and God wants us to look at them tenderly and love them just as they are, because each is a child of God, who is beloved and adored, and because Our Lord paid the price for their love with his blood. They are covered with Our Lord's blood like a coat, for the love of God and Jesus extend to all to the point of his being consumed for them in the sacrifice at Calvary (OS, 88–89).

I believe that there is no other Gospel teaching that had a more profound effect upon me and transformed my life more than the following: "All that you do to the least of these, you do to me." If we believe that these words are the words of the Incarnate Truth, those from the mouth which said "this is my body, this is my blood," with what strength we are driven to seek and love Jesus through these lesser ones, these sinners, these poor, by employing every material way as a means to soothe their temporal miseries (LLM, 210).

L ord Jesus, with true authority you proclaimed the new covenant and you advised us: "Love your enemies and pray for those who persecute you, so that you may be children of your Father in heaven; for he makes his sun rise on the evil and on the good, and sends rain on the righteous and on the unrighteous. For if you love those who love you, what reward do you have? Do not even the tax collectors do the same? And if you greet only your brothers and sisters, what more are you doing than others? Be perfect, therefore, as your heavenly Father is perfect" (Mt 5:44–48).

Lord Jesus, in this discourse, you show me that I should not pay attention to any of the barriers human beings erect concerning others. You call upon me to treat the one who I would not normally consider my brother or sister as such, in spite of differences in race, culture, and religion. You show me that this love for my neighbor extends all the way to my enemies. By acting according to your instructions, I will make myself a portrait of our Father in heaven. The more I love, the more I will be like him. May all be able to recognize him in me: such a Father, such a Son! Is this love not what we notice in Brother Charles's life and what drove his will to be "the universal brother"? Numerous times, he repeated these words: "To be the friend of all, both good and bad, is to be the universal brother" (CB, 115).

Brother Charles often reminded his future disciples about "their work of immense and universal charity." He said, "Lord Jesus, at the same time as you introduced this new practice concerning love of mankind to the world, you also introduced new reasons to love all mankind" (PFJ, 111). In order to love in accordance with this new law, it is essential for us to have a new outlook about others, one which goes beyond the surface, "a second sight," so to speak. Father Foucauld said, "To be able to truly see others, we must close our physical eyes and open the eyes of our souls. Let us see what they are from within, not what they appear to be. Let us look at them in the same way as God looks at them" (QPR, 41).

No matter what type of person is placed along our route, whether he is the most unfamiliar or whether he is "the last of the last" morally, is it not you, Jesus, that I should see in him? Change my heart and my outlook to become deeper in tune with you, for it is you I reach through my faith. Brother Charles admonishes us: We must receive "everyone, the poor Turk and the Bishop, everyone, and by receiving them, we receive Jesus" (PFJ, 37).

In order to be open to receiving all, we must endeavor to rise above, and this usually does not occur without some pain, instinctive reactions that have arisen out of aversions and malice. I admit that I feel more at ease with someone who has had a similar background to mine, who speaks the same language or holds the same convictions, someone who is a member of my group, of my Church, and it is easier to do this with my neighbor. The gospels oblige me to go beyond these spontaneous sympathies; if I do not, what more am I doing than "the pagans"? Lord Jesus, I beg you, in the words of Brother Charles, "to give us this new feeling, this second sight to always see you in each of your children so that we may be able to treat you, in each, like we should" (EJ, 126).

We should keep the spirit of witness ever present. Let us join in the confident statement of Father Peyriguère, the disciple of Brother Charles who said these words after spending the day tending to the sick: "Here, by caring for these children, I see Him, I touch Him. I have the physical sense of having touched the body of Christ. It is an extraordinary grace."

This fraternal love does not consist of good thoughts and nice words. At the end of all time, we will be judged by our actions: "I was hungry and you gave me food, I was thirsty and you gave me something to drink" (Mt 25:35). What are we doing to "soothe temporal miseries"? In this statement

Brother Charles was not speaking directly about the Third World but isn't that what he could have been thinking when he wrote: "We must be united with all our brothers, even the most marginalized. We must love them and invite them to unite with us, look at them as our brothers, and share our wealth with these less fortunate brothers who are scattered in the winds of heaven. Let us call them to us, let us fraternize with them" (QPR, 70–71)?

Lord, help us overcome all the obstacles on this difficult road to love our brothers, all our brothers! Let us stop labeling them at the risk of inhibiting the spark of our fraternal charity. Let us avoid, like the plague, all generalizations by attributing the collective faults, or the faults of a few, to all. Do not let us make the guilt of a crime committed by one of its members reflect upon the entire group. The Second Vatican Council reprobated this practice with respect to the Jewish people. Let us extend this respect to all. All generalizations commit an injustice which is the source of intolerance and racism.

Lord, you commanded that we not judge our neighbor: "Do not judge, so that you may not be judged." We are so easily prone to notice the faults of others, especially if we suffer from them ourselves, as in the lesson of the speck and the log. "You hypocrite, first take the log out of your own eye, and then you will see clearly to take the speck out of your neighbor's eye" (Mt 7:5). As Brother Charles points out: "If I have an uncharitable thought against my neighbor, then I have a similar thought against Our Lord himself, for he said: what you do to one of those little ones, you do to me" (DP, 256). To turn away from my brother by judging or ignoring him is to turn away from you, Lord! How can one pray in such a situation?

By taking Communion in your body that was given to us, and in your blood that was shed for us, I unite myself intensely to you, Lord Jesus. I unite myself with all those that you carry in yourself. To refuse my love to one of those human beings, near or far, is to break this unity that you hold so dear, it is to falsify my eucharistic Communion.

I must show solidarity; I must do it in many different ways, whether I want to or not. I must show solidarity with my co-workers, neighbors, compatriots, and with the faithful of my Church, and even with all the sinners of the world. I cannot pull myself from those bonds; and I would make a mistake if I mentally envisioned myself as apart from others or if I considered myself different by showing contempt for them as did the Pharisee in his prayer: "God, I thank you that I am not like other people: thieves, rogues, adulterers, or even like this tax collector" (Lk 18:11). Lord, I pray that I will never imitate the Pharisee and thus incur your wrath!

My solidarity with others would probably not hold fast if it were only based on feelings. Its roots stem from the contemplation of the mystery of the Holy Trinity. The unity that exists between you and your Father, Jesus, represents the ultimate model to imitate. Lord Jesus, was this not the meaning of your prayer on Holy Thursday evening? Brother Charles makes this point: "Just as the Father lives in the Son through love and just as the Son lives in the Father through the love he has for him, so, in this way, we must live in all mankind, through the love that we have for our brothers and sisters...and we must love them to the extent of living within them, through love, and not within ourselves. (…) Let them be one in us, and may it be our love for God that unites us, in this manner, to all mankind" (PFJ, 120–121).

Lord, when you taught us to pray by reciting the Our Father for the first time, you used the universal "us" of human solidarity. I only pray to our Father in heaven as a brother of all mankind and in the name of all peoples everywhere. I don't say "my," but "our" Father. I join with Brother Charles by saying these words: "When I ask for both the bread of grace and the Eucharist, I do not ask for myself alone, I ask for all mankind....I make no requests for myself alone. All that I ask for in the Father is either for God or for all mankind, for us all, the children of Our Lord, whom he loves, for us all who have been redeemed by his blood" (QPR, 102).

When Brother Charles appointed himself as an "older brother," he explained to his correspondent that loving one's neighbor is the royal road which leads to the love of God. "It is by loving humankind that we learn to love God." He returned to this same subject during the last year of his life, when he wrote: "In order to love God, love your fellow man. See a child of God, a brother of Jesus, in all humans....There is no better way to love God than by being charitable toward his children, so that he can see it" (LLM, 127, 197).

Lord, from the time you came to live among us, you proposed this way of love to men of good will, according to the gospel: "But those who do what is true come to the light, so that it may be clearly seen that their deeds have been done in God" (Jn 3:21). Lord Jesus, at the end of time, when you will be sitting in final judgment, you will bring "all nations" together, just as you say in the gospel. What a surprise the little-known saints will have through this marvelous revelation: "Truly I tell you, just as you did it to one of the least of these who are members of my family, you did it to me" (Mt 25:40). Dazzled and joyous, they will see Jesus in a way they had not discovered during their lives.

In order to be more convinced of what he was preaching, Brother Charles, in a meditation, reflects on what Jesus told him: "The best way to know if you are growing and progressing in divine love and in all virtues is to discover if you are growing in love for your neighbor and in humility....If you are growing in those two aspects, it is proof positive that you are growing toward perfection" (MSE, 267). These words echo Saint Paul's aphorism: "Owe no one anything, except to love one another; for the one who loves another has fulfilled the law....Love does no wrong to a neighbor; therefore, love is the fulfilling of the law" (Rom 13:8, 10).

In our desire to pray with Brother Charles, let us make his words our own: "Lord Jesus, since we are called to follow your example, and make our hearts become like God's heart, good and loving toward all people....Since we are called to follow your example, we must obey God, by not only doing good for the bodies and souls of our neighbors, but by doing it as he does it, and as you do it, O Jesus, lovingly and tenderly, by uniting our heart with, and changing our heart to be like, God's own heart. He asks this of us with such great love" (PPF, 24).

REFLECTION QUESTIONS

Do I have difficulties accepting people who are different from me? What is my relationship with family members and others who have offended me? Do I pray for openness toward others? Do I recognize the call of the gospel to go beyond the externals of people and places?

DAY TEN

God's Unexpected Roads

FOCUS POINT

Obedience to the call of God is radical love. When Jesus called the disciples, they left everything and followed him. Jesus said of himself, "I have come to do the will of him who sent me." We are called to imitate this same understanding of obedience in our lives. Christ was obedient unto death, even death on a cross.

Obedience is the last, highest, and most perfect degree of love. It is the degree in which we cease to exist for ourselves, when we die like Jesus died on the Cross, when we give the Beloved a lifeless body and soul, without a will, without any movement of its own, and with which he can do whatever he wants. That is most undoubtedly and certainly the highest degree of love. This degree encompasses all others, goes beyond all of them, is transcendent, beyond everything....

Let us not give our living selves to Our Lord, since he died for us. Let us give ourselves to him, as he gave himself for us, through death, in perfect obedience, without reservation. Perfect love is perfect obedience (LFT, 149–150).

It is not necessary to prepare oneself in advance in order to do great things: to glorify God in the most admirable way; to convert the world as the apostles did; to be the cornerstone and head of the Church like Saint Paul. No amount of preparation is necessary, not days, months, or years. The only thing that is necessary is to constantly obey God's orders (CM, 223).

To obey is to love. It is the purest, most perfect, highest, most selfless, and most adoring act of love. If I dare say so, to obey, mainly at the beginning, forces us to perform quite a few acts of mortification. After a certain amount of time, we see things as they really are, we become detached from everything (LFT, 145).

L ord Jesus, the beginning of your public life had as its setting the luminous charms of the lakeshore. The fishermen were at work when you called to them: "When they brought their boats to shore, they left everything and followed him" (Lk 5:11).

We admire this instant availability. It is with this in mind that Brother Charles noted that no amount of preparation for the decision to follow Jesus was necessary, not even a single minute, "the only thing that is necessary is to constantly obey God's orders." Agreed, but those hidden years that preceded this public affirmation, years undoubtedly invisibly guided by the Lord, had prepared the apostles for this decisive instant without their knowing it. A series of small positive replies lead to the great "yes." For Peter, this first calling marked the beginning of a story of friendship whose last episode would take place on these same shores with the thrice-asked question: "Do you love me?"

In effect, love is at the root of true obedience which is altogether different from the obedience of a slave. One just has to look at you, Lord Jesus, to see this difference. Brother Charles constantly brings us back to his ideal of imitating you, most especially in the virtue of obedience. He says: "Obedience is the first accomplishment of love, just as our Lord Jesus demonstrated through the example of this life and the strength of his words: 'I have not come to do my own will, but that of the One who has sent me,' 'Whoever loves me will follow my commandments,' and 'Whoever acts, at all times, in perfect obedience, acts in perfect love, at all times'" (MSE, 518). Lord, a few hours before your death, when you told your apostles: "I do as the Father has commanded me, so that the world may know that I love the Father" (Jn 14:31), you, once again, were referring to the link between obedience and love. And to better underline this profound life-giving element of your life, you used a comparison with food: "My food is to do the will of him who sent me and to complete his work" (Jn 4:34). We cannot live without food. This shows us just how essential obedience is: it made Jesus stand tall, it propelled him all the way to the cross! One day, a friend echoed your words, Lord, and although his frankness took nothing away from his generosity toward you, he complained in his prayer: "I accept the fact that I must do your will, my Lord, but I must admit that this food is not always very appetizing!" I can only imagine your smile, Lord.

When you taught us to pray, you revealed the theme of your conversations with your Father, who is also our own: "Our Father." And at the heart of this prayer comes the phrase that transcends everything else, the ardent desire that "Thy will be done." During the dark hours of Holy Thursday, this request will change into a painful supplication on your lips, and drops of your blood will stain the earth. How can we, now that our turn has come, repeat or even chant this prayer without seeking, with all our strengths and weaknesses, to accomplish your will each and every day?

No human being could demand such an unconditional type of submission as has been described by Brother Charles. If I conform to it, it could only be to obey God. In the religious life, in particular, in convents and monasteries, an overseer, a superior, or an authority could be the intermediary to show us God's will. And if I carry out his request, it is only because I accept it, in spite of its human limitations, as an expression of God's will.

But most of us are not members of a religious order. Even for them, in their daily lives, as in our own, rarely are we subjected to precise orders, even less so to a visit from an angel to show the way on God's behalf. Then, how will we know God's will? This reflection from Pascal gives an admirable answer: "If God created experts in his will, then they would have to obey generously: necessity and events in our life are infallibly these experts."

One can only imagine Brother Charles in constant observance of his Rule. A meticulous man, he organized his day right down to the smallest of details. However, unforseen events undoubtedly occur to upset everything. In Beni-Abbès, in spite of the regimented cloistered lifestyle, people and events monopolized his time, destroyed his plans, and changed his ideas. They soon forced him to leave "the nest" and travel along desert roads toward the unknown. How did he react to these unexpected events, and can his attitude inspire our own and guide our prayers?

We see Brother Charles adapt himself to events without resistance. Numerous times, he said: "I will do what I judge to be best according to circumstances" (LMB, 30). When he received permission to leave the Trappists, had he not already written: "God leads us down such unexpected roads. See how I have been led and bounced around over the last six months: Staouéli, Rome, and now the unknown. We are the dry leaf, the grain of dust, the speck of sea foam which are carried by the whim of the wind. Let us be no more and no less than faithful; let ourselves be carried, with great love and obedience, to where God's will takes us...until the very last breath of this blessed wind carries us to heaven" (LFT, 153)? Let us remember this enlightenment: God steers us; encounters and events are his messengers. As a true daughter of Brother Charles, Little Sister Magdeleine confided: "God took me by the hand and, blindly, I followed."

Brother Charles gave up the idea of being the master of his own future when he first wrote, in 1903: "I live one day at a time" (LMB, 118), and in the following year: "I live day by day, striving only to do God's will every minute of the day" (LHC, 156), and again: "Day by day, I strive to do the will of Jesus and I enjoy great inner peace" (LMB, 146). Brother Charles also said: "Let us concern ourselves only with the present and not worry about the future, living as if the world is going to end today." And he added: "Sometimes, often, almost always, preparation for the future is done by us, but never on our own...never, because we want it for ourselves, always, because we only want the accomplishment of God's will at the present moment" (OS, 156).

To fully live this spirituality of the present moment, we are all called to follow this infallible recipe for holiness. Without casting a nostalgic glance back on an embellished past, where it may seem that our life was more fervent, and without worrying about the future, let us welcome all the richness of the present moment. Brother Charles quotes Father de Caussade as recommending: "All the work toward our sanctification consists of accepting, from one moment to the next, the sorrows and duties of the state as if they are veils which both hide and show God."

Father de Caussade's book, *Abandonment to Divine Providence*, was a book that highly influenced Brother Charles. This work, along with those of Saint Thérèse of Lisieux, are the only ones recommended by name in Brother Charles's Directory. He had, in fact, written to Massignon about *Abandonment to Divine Providence*: "The whole book is enlightening and elevates the soul" (LLM, 84).

The influence of this spiritual master also shows in some of Brother Charles's meditations. When Charles compares the Beloved's little brother, abandoned to divine will, to the dry leaf carried by the wind, he echoes Father de Caussade, who gave these instructions: "In the state of abandonment, the only rule is that of the present moment; then the soul is as light as a feather, fluid like water, as uncomplicated as a child."

How can we find the richness of the present moment when a time of temptation occurs? Brother Charles invites us to a positive outlook: "Each temptation is a blessing," he says. "God strengthens our love through the constant battle for his love. He makes us humble. He teaches us, makes us careful for ourselves, and generous toward others." Brother Charles continues: Through each of our spiritual battles, each of our trials and our sufferings, the Lord receives from us "a daily declaration of love…not only a declaration but a declaration with proof" (LLM, 59).

Some of the events of our life, whether they are important or not, do not say anything on their own, or may even suggest conflicting messages. Discernment, as put forth by our freedom, is not easy: we cannot expect a celestial fax to send us clear answers. We all need the support of a fraternal glance, the support of a team or a spiritual advisor in order to be able to interpret what is happening to us. If we call upon the Holy Spirit, then enlightenment will be there: God will always, in his own time, make his will known to the one who is seeking it. Brother Charles advises "the help of a wise spiritual director in order to better hear the voice of the Holy Spirit" (MSE, 500), but he also says that "when, in spite of our good intentions in questioning this spiritual director, we don't get the desired answers, God will enlighten us with the illumination of the Holy Spirit through reason and through the Gospel" (QPR, 293).

Lord, at every moment you lead me down roads you yourself have traced for my freedom. By analyzing all that happens to me, whether it is good or bad, inspire me to discover the incomparable wealth of the present moment, even if it upsets my plans or risks discouraging me. In the dark of night or the light of day, let me be convinced that you are extending your arms to me and that you are close to me in order to share my suffering or my joy: through me, you make them your own. Make it so that I am constantly ready to answer "yes" to your calls. Let us pray with Brother Charles: "My Father, arrange it so that your will be done in me and in all your creatures. Amen."

REFLECTION QUESTIONS

Do you see the unexpected in your life as a call from God? Do you find it difficult to live one day at a time? Do you find it difficult being in the present moment? Do you have a spiritual director? How well do you use the opportunity of spiritual direction? Have you ever thought about a regular spiritual director?

Master of the Impossible

FOCUS POINT

Prayer is familiarity with God. If we decide to live the inner call of the gospel, prayer is a most important practice. As we meditate on the gospels, we pattern our lives on that of Jesus, who often went away to pray.

To pray is to speak to God. To pray is to praise God. To pray is to tell God that we love him. To pray is to contemplate God. To pray is to have the spirit and the heart connected to God. To pray is to ask forgiveness from God. To pray is to call God to help us. To pray is to ask God for holiness and salvation for ourselves and all mankind....Love requires that we say that we love and that we repeat it in all its forms and that we praise what we love endlessly, without measure....Therefore, prayer cannot be separated from love, to the point that our prayers will become a type of measurement of our love (EJ, 76–77).

As humans, we are sensitive, we are capable of feeling, so thus we cannot shy away from or avoid pain....In our prayers, let us not hide our suffering from God...let us not be afraid to complain about them. On the contrary, let us reveal them, simply, with an open heart, as a son would to his Father, let us reveal them as would a loving heart that has an overwhelming need to confide everything it feels to the object of its passionate love...and let us call upon God to help us, for we like to call upon the one we love for help and we like to constantly receive help from him (EJ, 60–61).

What is impossible to humans is possible for God: "Caritas omnia sperat" (charity hopes for everything). God loves and can do anything. He respects the freedom he gave to mankind, but he does not hold back when he freely gives graces. His grace can be such that it overturns all obstacles and brings the calm after the storm. Let us know how to obtain powerful graces from the one who said: "Ask and you shall receive" and "When two or more of you are gathered in prayer, I am among you" (OS, 728).

Lord Jesus, we thank you for having shared with us your prayer in the garden of Gethsemani, where you appeared to be so utterly human. Jesus "knelt down, and prayed. 'Father, if you are willing, remove this cup from me; yet, not my will but yours be done.' ...In his anguish he prayed more earnestly, and his sweat became like great drops of blood falling down on the ground" (Lk 22:42, 44).

Lord Jesus, through these words, which have been repeated numerous times, you gave us the perfect example of a prayer.

In your prayer that night we see the two qualities of prayer brought to their culmination: your request, in the midst of your distress, a request so spontaneous, so like a scream or a call for help, together with your acceptance of the will of your Father. This acceptance is given with such total submission that you would come to renounce your very request, obliterating it with all your being through your filial acceptance of the chalice of the passion—accepting true death before death.

O Jesus, by meditating upon that supreme moment, Brother Charles explains to us that there are two ways of praying. The first: "Let your heart cry out, in a childlike simplicity, let it ask God for everything it wants…for itself and for others…and always end it with these words: 'not my will, but yours.'" The other way to pray "is to simply say the ending: 'My Father, may your will be done in this, whatever it may be.' Jesus gave us an example of the first way in the garden of Gethsemani. He gave us the example of the second way in the Our Father" (MSE, 245).

Jesus, by praying as you did, if I express an intense desire, if I beg for the healing of a loved one, if I cry out in pain, if I ask for light on the road to follow, I do it with a childlike simplicity, but also with the deep respect of a believer who does not see God as a vending machine of graces and who does not see prayer as the coinage that activates this machine every time.

God is God. He is not a "means" put at my disposal, brought down to my human level for the purpose of my personal needs, or even to guarantee the success of an apostolate undertaken for Him. God, the Almighty, remains transcendent. Faced with God's mystery, I am a shortsighted creature who is unaware of his will and who must let God guide him down the road. In the eyes of divine knowledge, all of us are all illiterates. That is why our first action must be one of adoration in which we express our feelings of admiration, unconditional submission, and preacceptance of his will, whatever it may be. Any demand we bring to him has no meaning unless it respects this fundamental attitude of recognition of God for what he is. Let there be no request unless it is clothed with adoration, whether it is spoken or not, before or after it.

Lord, in the prayer you taught us, you seek to elicit these feelings first. From the beginning, the words, "who art in heaven," look to "lift my soul very high, above this poor earth." And when I repeat after you, "hallowed be thy name, thy kingdom come," I try, with all my heart, to make those essential desires my own and, compared to them, my own request becomes relative.

Once my request is put in proper perspective, I can then freely ask, on everyone's behalf, for "our daily bread." As Brother Charles says: "Let us repeat our request two, three, or ten times without adding any new words or phrases, but letting our heart cry out freely and by adding, only from time to time, the words: 'however, not my will, but yours be done'" (EJ, 59). Brother Charles also says that in the expression of our desires, let us have the audacity of a child: "Let us not place a measure on our desires, since God has not put any on the power of our prayers, just as there is none on his goodness and his power" (EJ, 54).

Lord Jesus, your prayer on Holy Thursday evening was not fulfilled. Albeit, it was the most filial that could ever been said. O mysterious and unfathomable will of God! O Jesus, by contemplating you, as you were kneeling, faced with this divine silence, I draw certain comfort for those nights of discouragement when I feel that I have prayed in vain because a pressing desire, which sprung from a confident heart, remained unanswered. Brother Charles told us: "Let us believe that God will grant us everything that we ask for with faith. He will give it to us because he is infinitely good and all-powerful: he will grant it to us either by giving us the very thing we requested or by giving us something better. If he makes us wait, if we receive it late or not at all, be sure that the wait is what is best for us" (MSE, 197).

Lord, whatever happens, I believe that you are "the master of the impossible," and I remain unshakably convinced that the tenderness of a God who loves me madly endlessly surrounds me. Even in the dark of night, my hope keeps vigil like a small lamp: "Hope is faith in goodness," says Brother Charles. "Let us always have hope for everything, since the foundation of our hope is divine goodness" (LLM, 125).

At times, Lord, I will stand before you silently, with nothing to ask of you. And in my selfless adoration, I will give you proof that I did not come to you because I wanted something from you, but I did so simply because I love you. Brother Charles reminds us: "As Saint Thérèse of Lisieux told us, to pray is not to speak a great deal, but to love a great deal" (EJ, 26).

Lord, for some of us, prayer may constitute an escape to a false sense of peace, which would make us immune to the needs of our brothers. May we never hang this sign over the doors of our chapels: "Do not disturb, we are praying." Tomorrow will be too late to say: "Lord, if only I had known that it was you who was knocking at the door." Is it possible to say that the Lord is disturbing us, even when he comes in the guise of a needy person calling us?

Lord, others among us are so taken by what they see as such indispensable activities that they don't have any time for prayer, and, making excuses, can have illusions about their generosity. Lord, arrange it so that we can tell when our behavior conceals cowardice. One can escape in work as well as in prayer.

Let us show loyalty when called to serve our brothers and sisters. I know that problems, at times, are so great that we feel powerless. At those times, prayer becomes action. If we have expended every effort within our power, using all the means within our reach without solving our problem, "then," says Brother Charles, "our only recourse is prayer, which is more powerful than all other means. We must never act without praying, nor pray without taking action when we have the means to take action" (MSE, 503).

We can prayer with Brother Charles: "My God, replace this storm of passions, distractions, and temptations that is in my soul by a reverent silence where only your voice can be heard….In that profound silence, inform me of your will so that I can do it. That is my greatest need, O My Lord. Inform me, not only of your will, but also of what you are, because the better I know you, the more I will love you. Amen" (CFA, 272).

REFLECTION QUESTIONS

What is the quality of my prayer? Brother Charles offers many suggestions about how to pray. He presents to us the many ways we can cry out to God again and again. What feelings come up in you about prayer? Are the suggestions of Brother Charles helpful?

DAY TWELVE

The Eucharist Is Jesus Giving Himself

FOCUS POINT

The Eucharist is the source of our Christian life. In the Eucharist we are invited to experience the depth of Christ's love for us. The promise of Jesus that he would be with us always until the end of time is fulfilled in the reception of holy Communion. We are called through this union to become the presence of Jesus. We are called to be nourishment for others, especially those who are lonely and abandoned by the Church and by society.

What happiness! God is with us, God is in us, our God in whom we are and act, God who is close to us in the Tabernacle. O my God, what more do we need? How happy we are! Emmanuel, "God with us," these are, for all intents and pur-

poses, the first words of the Gospel...and the last words are "I will be with you until the end of time." How happy we are! How good you are! (MSE, 174).

The Eucharist is Jesus, it is all Jesus! My Beloved Jesus, you are whole and alive in the Eucharist, as fully as you were in the home of the Holy Family in Nazareth...as fully as you were amidst your Apostles. In the same way, you are here, my Beloved and my All (MSE, 174).

You are here, Lord Jesus. How close you are, my God, my Savior, my Jesus, my brother, my Spouse, my Beloved. It would be foolish to believe that there is a better way to achieve this glory than to be at his feet....Let us love him as much as possible, that is all we need for eternity....When we love, we feel that none of the time spent with our beloved is lost. It is a time most well spent, except when the will and the well-being of our beloved calls us elsewhere (DP, 81–83).

"Take, eat; this is my body....Drink, all of you; for this is my blood" (Mt 26:26–28). *How the infinite grace of the Holy Eucharist must make us love a God who is so good, so close to us, so totally with us, and in us; how the grace of the Eucharist must make us love the beauty and supreme perfection of the one who gives himself to us, who comes inside us. There is no explanation needed; it is obvious....How the Holy Eucharist must make us kind and good toward all mankind. This is also obvious: how could the tongue that has touched God speak anything but words that are worthy of divine charity? How can the soul that has received God conceive thoughts which do not conform to God's goodness? How can the body in which God has sojourned commit acts that are unworthy of the gentle-*

ness of its divine inhabitant? Should not this being in whom
God has made his dwelling, his temple, overflow with the good-
ness of its celestial guest? (PPF, 93–94).

———

Lord Jesus, the disciples were gathered on the mountain in
Galilee for their farewells. You said to them: "And remember, I am with you always, to the end of the age" (Mt 28:20).
Then, with this promise, your blessed voice ceased to exist on
our earth. Even though Jesus' earthly presence has passed,
Brother Charles reminds us that the Eucharist is, first and foremost, his presence with us every day, a presence which extends, in sacramental form, the mystery of the Incarnation.
The Eucharist, he says, "is God with us, God in us." And we
can understand that Brother Charles's ardent faith in this real
presence would elicit these words from him: "To adore the
Holy Host, that should be the foundation of every human's
life" (OS, 399).

The adoration of the Holy Sacrament is an intimate and
selfless time since it is a time of love. When I go into the chapel,
it is not because I need to, or because I was drawn there, it is
because I love. Lord, in the darkness of faith, maybe even in
dry spells, I persevere by giving you time which, to humans,
would seem to be as wasteful as that "pound of costly per-
fume made of pure nard" (Jn 12:3) which was poured on your
feet. Will we hear your reply: "Leave her alone. She bought it
so that she might keep it for the day of my burial. You always
have the poor with you, but you do not always have me" (Jn
12:7–8). Will this reply be heard by those who feel that this
time would have been better spent at a more "profitable" ac-
tivity?

Brother Charles wants his future brothers and sisters to be dedicated to the perpetual adoration of the holy Sacrament. Whatever their occupation, he sees them, hour after hour "with their eyes fixed on the Holy Host as if it were in the holy home in Nazareth between the Blessed Virgin and Saint Joseph, constantly gazing at Jesus, our older brother, and striving...to melt themselves into Him in an almost always more perfect unity. It is a unity for which our earthly and all-too-human love has an unquenchable thirst" (RD, 110).

The unity of which Brother Charles speaks is realized, mysteriously but truly, through the eucharistic Communion, which is prepared and perpetuated by those long hours of adoration at the foot of the altar. "Those who eat my flesh and drink my blood abide in me, and I in them" (Jn 6:56). Jesus, you want us to have this "real food," which unites us with you. And you compare this unity to the unity between you and your Father. How astonishing it is to believe that those sublime instants of unity which, for Brother Charles, evoked marriage, can occur in the mundane company of routine and distractions! Nevertheless, the true Sacrament takes place in spite of our mediocrity. Lord, I do not wish to criticize you, but what a monumental risk you took when you put yourself into our sinful hands in the form of an ordinary piece of bread. From you, this can only have been done with the full knowledge of its consequences. Love is made up of such foolishness.

Jesus, in this meeting, we are nourished through a "condition" like your own. How do you appear to me in the Eucharist? You are there under the infinitely humble form of bread and wine, and you do nothing to impose yourself upon me or to seduce me. You wait for me to make the first move, freely, with confidence in your word upon which I rely totally. Oh, that impressive silence of the Eucharist! Then, living off your life, I bring this humble and silent presence to my brothers, which is enlivened by the same divine respect and love that you show us. The tone of my witness, as well as the intensity of my fraternal charity, stem from the Eucharist.

You are present, not like an inert object, regardless of how precious this object may be, but like a living being, through the very act of giving yourself to save the world. You have said: "This is my blood which has been shed for you and all of mankind." Will this not change our outlook about our brothers who, like us, have also celebrated that mystical marriage? Brother Charles says: "What devotion we must have for the bodies and souls of all those Christians who, through Holy Communion, have been so intimately united with Jesus...who have been his spouses, his temples, in such a marvelous way. How we must hold these bodies and souls dear, precious, and sacred" (PFJ, 67).

Communion does not only transform our outlook, but also our heart, which becomes one with the heart of Jesus, from which we gain an impetus that leads us to give ourselves to our brothers in a thousand different ways. Our actions, fueled by holy Communion, prolong Jesus' own gift of himself to all our brothers through us. From the "temple" that we are, "the goodness of our celestial guest" overflows like water from a spring.

Brother Charles is happy to light the lamps of the tabernacles across the Sahara; that is to say, he multiplies the presence of the Eucharist amidst people who do not know the Lord Jesus. He places the region where he resides under the care of the Eucharist, saying: "Each day that I can celebrate the Holy Sacrifice, the Holy Host takes possession of its realm" (OS, 675). He gave us this reflection in 1904 when he took a few days rest in the middle of a long trip to Tamanrasset. He was very happy because "a chapel was built out of branches and was crowned with a wooden cross." He exclaimed: "Sacred Heart of Jesus, thank you for this first tabernacle in the country of the Tuaregs! May it be the prelude to many others....Sacred Heart of Jesus, may you radiate from this tabernacle upon the people around you who do not know you" (CB, 144). This radiance of the Host, spreading out over a whole country, represents, for Brother Charles, a spiritual geography superimposed over the visible landscape. To see the holy Sacrament installed in this place is as meaningful to him as was our Lord's choice to live in Nazareth and not somewhere else.

This concept of the Incarnation does not necessarily imply some magical concept of the real presence. Furthermore, this champion of the Eucharist knows that charity is supreme. His devotion to the holy Sacrament, like his prayers, evolved through his lifetime. If his meditations from Tamanrasset, close to the end of his life, had been written in the same way as those from Nazareth, which he wrote ten years earlier, we would be better able to appreciate the difference in his spiritual tones from those two periods.

In 1900, when he was living in Nazareth and thinking about entering the priesthood, he felt that "just one Mass offered to God is infinitely better than any other work I could do." Seven years later, he asked himself: "Is it better to go to Hoggar and not be able to celebrate Mass (for the lack of company) or not go and be able to celebrate Mass?" He was the only priest who could go to those southern oases and "silently bring Jesus to those who don't know him." His passion for the salvation of souls, through the imitation of Jesus, took him "always further down the road" and forced him to give up celebrating Mass as long as he was not authorized to celebrate it alone.

Brother Charles explained to his bishop: "Before, I was inclined to see the infinite, the Holy Sacrifice, from one aspect, and the finite, everything that is not him, from another. I was inclined to always sacrifice everything else in favor of celebrating the Holy Mass. But this reasoning must be faulty in some way because the Apostles, the greatest saints, sacrificed the possibility of celebrating Mass, on many occasions, in favor of doing other spiritual work of charity" (OS, 695).

Lord Jesus, your love for all my brothers is infinite. They are also your brothers and I live among them. You give your life for them through the Eucharist. You want to love them and give them life through me. Let us pray with Brother Charles: "Enlighten, guide, save those souls you love....Convert me, as sinful as I am, Sacred Heart of Jesus" (CB, 144–145).

REFLECTION QUESTIONS

Brothers Charles's experience of the Eucharist may be an invitation to us to consider our understanding of this mystery of faith. How do you experience the Eucharist? What thoughts and desires go through your mind during the Eucharist? In what ways do you live the mystery of the Eucharist in your daily life? Does the Eucharist open your eyes to see Jesus in those around you?

DAY THIRTEEN

The Heart and the Cross

FOCUS POINT

The life of Jesus shows us the face of God. In the Eucharist we are given the presence of Jesus in our lives and through his passion, death, and Resurrection, we are invited into the mystery of Christ. We are invited through these mysteries to share in God's love for us and for all of creation.

Lord, you give up your spirit and say, "It is finished" (Jn 19:30). It is finished because you gave us everything, your humanity and your divinity. Through thirty-three years of examples and teachings, you gave us all that you are in the Holy Eucharist. You gave us your blood through your Passion, and you gave us your mother when you were on the Cross. In just one instant of your life…you gave us everything….So now, it is finished. Your labor of love is finished, you loved mankind "until the end," until the end of what was feasible through the Incar-

nation and the Holy Eucharist, until the end of your life, right to the last drop of your blood....O Heart of Jesus, which was pierced for us, how you love us! (MSE, 518).

I hear Jesus saying: "Religion is my Heart: it is my Heart because when you see it, you are reminded of God's love and of the love you should have for God....My Heart wants to be yours eternally. It wants you to be transformed and, in some way, deified in it. Such is God's love for you, infinite through the infinite good he wants for you, of which you are reminded by my Heart. (...) Religion is expressed completely in the word love, caritas" (EJ, 261).

Sacred Heart of Jesus, thank you for giving me, through the suffering you endured for me, such proof of love that, from now on, I am compelled to have an unshakable confidence in your love, I am compelled to have eternal hope....O Heart of Jesus, regardless of my infidelities, my ingratitude, and negligence toward you and my sins against you, after seeing the proof you gave me of your love, I will always believe in your constant, faithful, and unshakable love for me. I will always believe that I only have to come back to you and you will be ready to forgive me...ready to greet me as the father greeted the prodigal son...that you will be ready to help me with your divine strength and with more desire than even the most ardent human heart, and so, for the rest of my life, I am prepared to do what pleases you the most....O Heart of Jesus, I thank you (EJ, 179–180).

I see the prodigal son setting out on the road to return to his father's house. Lord Jesus, you described this memorable scene so admirably for us: "But while he was still far off, his father saw him and was filled with compassion; he ran and put his arms around him and kissed him" (Lk 15:20).

The father was holding vigil—the son was not aware of that, for the son could not imagine such tenderness. It was the father who ran to embrace and kiss his child. We are right to say that this parable is about the father's love. Could no prophet, before Jesus, have conceived of such an image of God as so compassionate and forgiving? To perceive that God is "like that" is beyond the realm of the most penetrating of human intelligence. Such an extraordinary and astonishing revelation could only come from God himself.

Through the words and the life of Jesus, we discover a yet unknown face of God. Jesus is the road to that discovery. Does he not repeat to us: "He who sees me, sees the Father"? Does he not say: "What my Father has given me is greater than all else, and no one can snatch it out of the Father's hand. The Father and I are one" (Jn 10:29–30)? We can safely say with Father Gay that "Christ's heart is the revelation of God's heart, the cross is the revelation of Christ's heart."

We must remember that "God so loved the world that he gave his only Son, so that everyone who believes in him may not perish but may have eternal life" (Jn 3:16). And this Son, God's living image on earth, loved all the way to his death on the cross, and there, he said: "It is finished."

In his Rule, Brother Charles meticulously stated that his Little Brothers and Sisters would wear on their chests a red fabric heart which is crowned with a cross—"the heart and the cross will measure 15 cm in height"—because "his divine Heart is a model for their own and the emblem of their mission." A heart, not one pierced with an arrow, but pierced with a cross, the price of the love it symbolizes.

This symbol alone does not speak on its own to those we meet. It represents a love that comes from God which can only radiate through us. It commits us to manifest this divine love toward all mankind. Brother Charles says thus: "The fraternities of the Sacred Heart are small hearths of love where the Sacred Heart of Jesus burns. They are hearths which are located, for the most part, in mission countries, in order to 'light the fire that Jesus brought to earth' and radiate the flames of the divine Heart on its most unfortunate children, the most lost..." (RD, 106–107). For Brother Charles, to respond to the Sacred Heart's love with our own love implies that we also love our brothers at the same time: "The emblem of Jesus' heart reminds you that you must give God the same love he gives you...and that you must love your neighbor as yourself, in the eyes of God, who loves everyone...because God loves him as he loves you" (EJ, 261). Brother Charles consistently comes back to stress these two intertwined commandments and their inseparable connection.

To say that a Christian is, above all, someone who loves God is a far from complete definition. Other believers, and especially mystics, strive to love God with all their hearts. As for ourselves, we are disappointed when, examining our conscience, we find that we love God so poorly. Are we not putting too much emphasis on ourselves? For, as one of Brother Charles's disciples so vigorously stressed, what defines a Christian is not that he loves God, but that he believes that God loves him.

This conviction calls for a redirection of one's outlook. Instead of looking at our sins and our limitations, and at the lukewarmness of our love, we should lift our heads and look to the Lord and repeat: "Lord, it's wonderful that you love me." This "conversion," which refocuses us away from ourselves, make us turn from "I" toward "you." You are what's important, your love is so certain and so blinding we can see nothing else. May we hear you always whisper to us: "Look at me as you work for me, as you pray, constantly" (DP, 130).

To entangle myself in the discovery of my shortcomings, my temptations, my stumblings, makes me slip back into doubt and discouragement. Thus, in my confusion, I echo Peter's words: "Go away from me, Lord, for I am a sinful man!" (Lk 5:8). Lord, while believing myself to be unfit for your love, I nevertheless believe, that in certain circumstances when I feel that I could be satisfactory, I am worthy of your love. Isn't that ridiculous? Lord, do such ideas displease you, or do they make you smile benevolently? Brother Charles reminds us: "If he only accepted those who are worthy of him, whom would he accept? Is he not the lover of our souls, seeking their love first and foremost?" (LLM, 113). You love me because of what you are, and you love me as I am. Lord, arrange it so that this belief dwells in me, firmly rooted, even through the darkest days, for as Brother Charles says: "He loves us because he is good, not because we are good—do not mothers love even their delinquent children?" (LLM, 206).

You set out to find your lost lamb and you anxiously await the return of the prodigal son. And from the cross—it is no longer a parable—you shorten the set procedure, you canonize the good bandit through a gesture of love from your Sacred Heart. After your Resurrection, you asked Peter for only a little love: when he denied you, you remained faithful. That is not very logical, is it? Only love can explain such behavior. And it forces me to have blind trust, as blind as that love is foolish, even if I come before you "empty-handed," as Thérèse of Lisieux used to say. This feeling permeates my prayer of thanksgiving, recognition, and marvel, in the same way as Brother Charles who lavished his meditations with thousands of thank you's. Let us say with him: "O my God, how good you are, thank you, thank you!"

Now let us join Brother Charles in praying: "Since you are always with us through your love and through your Heart, we should always be with you in ours. May our heart beat only for you. May all of our thoughts, words, and actions be inspired by your love in such a way that they will be the most pleasing to your heart as possible" (MSE, 174).

REFLECTION QUESTIONS

In his life, Brother Charles came to a deep faith in the paschal mystery. He experienced a profound conversion which enabled him to experience the mysteries of faith. Is your faith vibrant and alive? Are you in a place of spiritual dryness? How do the insights of Brother Charles's experience connect with your own spiritual experience?

DAY FOURTEEN
Our Master's Last Prayer

FOCUS POINT

Brother Charles was driven by the desire to imitate the life and virtues of Jesus in his life. Gradually, through his prayer and reflection on the gospels, his life took on the attitudes of Jesus, especially in his surrender to the will of the Father. His life is an example of how one can pattern his or her own life on the life of Jesus. In this respect, Brother Charles captured the heart of the teachings of Saint Paul.

"Father, into your hands I commend my spirit" (Lk 23:46) was our Beloved Master's last prayer. May it be ours. And may it not only be our prayer at the very end of our life, but throughout our lifetime. Father, into your hands I commend myself; Father, I trust in you; Father, I give myself up to you; Father, do with me as you please; and I thank you regardless of what you do with me. Thank you for everything; I am ready for

anything, I accept everything, I thank you for everything. In as much as your will is done in me, Lord, in as much as your will is done in your creatures, in all your children, in all those whom your heart loves, I want nothing else. Lord, into your hands I commend my soul. I give it to you with all the love of my heart because I love you. Out of my need for love comes my desire to give myself to you, to commend myself into your hands without measure. Into your hands, I commend myself with infinite trust because you are my Father (EJ, 88–89).

If persecution, the possibility of martyrdom, sickness, or the vision of death knocks at the door, may it rekindle our desire to give ourselves up so that we may meet Jesus. May this desire flame up ever higher and brighter. Persecution, sickness, and danger are, for us, a call, like the chimes of the clock that used to make Saint Thérèse shiver with joy and think: "Another hour less to be separated from Jesus" and "My Spouse is coming." It is the hope that we shall soon be united for eternity where it will be impossible for us to offend, displease, or stop loving and adoring Jesus...united with the only One we love who is our whole life, our whole desire, our everything, our whole love (RD, 309).

I must live today as if I were to die a martyr tonight (SAD, 113).

———

L ord, your last cry when you were on the Cross was heard through the centuries, well beyond that darkest hour on Good Friday: "It was now about noon, and darkness came over the whole land until three in the afternoon, while the sun's light failed; and the curtain of the temple was torn in two. Then Jesus, crying with a loud voice, said, 'Father, into your hands I commend my spirit.' Having said this, he breathed his last" (Lk 23:44–46).

Lord, your supreme prayer, when you were alone and abandoned on the cross brings an end to that terrible supplication begun at Gethsemani. In it, you proclaim your total abandonment, your perfect submission to your Father's will. "Father, may your will be done"; isn't this formula, which you have taught us, at the heart of any prayer, the heart of all Christian life?

Brother Charles, in his meditation, explained your last words in a few moving phrases in order to help us profoundly share the feelings that were condensed in so few words. His explanation so closely corresponds to his inner feelings that, through it, we can recognize the essential basis for his life of unity with his Beloved. These lines have become Father de Foucauld's prayer of abandonment to which his disciples strive to adhere, with all their being, by repeating it over and over.

Lord Jesus, you carry all our trials in your heart. All our painful cries converge in your Good Friday proclamation. All our acceptances join your supreme prayer.

At times, my being rebels, and I am incapable of saying phrases such as: "I am ready for everything; I accept it all." In theory, I am able to admit the truth these words transmit but I hesitate to make them clearly my own. It appears to be beyond my power to go forward toward the future in this way with my eyes closed. If the truth be told, this frightens me: if the Lord takes me at my word, how my imagination can run amuck! And yet all that is needed is to walk in your footsteps, Lord, and to take your hand. As Father de Caussade says: "When we are led by a guide who takes us to an unknown land, at night, through fields, without a clear path, do we have any other choice than abandonment?"

Lord, I find that to be in your care, as docile as a cadaver, is rather macabre. It is true that the entire ascetic tradition uses this same comparison as did Brother Charles in his Trappist prayers. Lord, we have become too familiar with the terms that you used because they do not put any demands on us. You expect your disciples to renounce themselves, that they be like some who would lose their lives in the same way as it is postulated in the gospel: "If any want to become my followers, let them deny themselves and take up their cross and follow me. For those who want to save their life will lose it, and those who lose their life for my sake, and for the sake of the gospel, will save it" (Mk 8:34–35).

Lord, to resign oneself to the acceptance of "losing one's life" by following this example requires a foolish trust in you, wrote Jean Ploussard, a spiritual follower of Brother Charles: "Far from hating or fleeing from life, I have a foolish passion for it. I have found that everything God has made is beautiful, good, and well made and I loudly proclaim that there is only one reason to renounce it: his Word. This is infinitely disconcerting because it is far beyond our own logic....Allah Akbar, that is everything."

Our Muslim brothers use Abraham who, in good faith, believed that God wanted him to sacrifice his only son, as a model for abandonment and submission. Was this child not the promised one? Didn't God appear to contradict himself? To human eyes, that seems to be a cruel absurdity. The "father of the believers" bowed down without hesitation and announced his "here I am" that millions of believers have echoed after him. To submit oneself in this way, in the darkness of night, at times requires a type of heroism that is not within our power. By repeating each phrase of the prayer of abandonment, I add to it an ardent call to the Lord so that, from within myself, I will be able to adhere, without restrictions, to what I am reciting. May my words become even truer each day.

Without fear, I will push ahead on the path which this prayer has opened for me, because a luminous certainty has transformed it "with infinite confidence because you are my Father," a Father who loves me as inexplicably as the prodigal's father. When I add that last phrase, that act of trust, to the affirmations which, without it, would seem terrifying, it reminds me of a dark alley in my neighborhood, which, when illuminated every night by large light standards, brings each house out of the darkness. I must say: "Yes, I am ready for anything, I accept everything with infinite trust, because you are my Father."

When I say, perhaps painfully: "No matter what you do to me, I thank you," these simple words change into a declaration of love for the One who loved me first. As de Caussade reminds us: "The act of abandonment is nothing other than an act of love."

Things that happen to me sometimes outrage me or force me to ask unanswerable questions, and my acceptance becomes a battle. Brother Charles describes it as "a battle undertaken through love...a proof of pure love, an act of love in the dark of night, in the face of the appearance of desertion, in the face of self-doubt, and in all the bitterness of love with none of its sweetness" (LLM, 67).

Father, why don't you answer our cries of distress, our declarations of love which are, at times, painfully extracted from our will? It is true that you, Jesus, felt this feeling of abandonment. "My God, my God, why have you forsaken me?" you ask in Matthew 27:46. We are faced with the same wall of silence as you experienced. I am not the only one to complain of this. Brother Charles also noted in his workbook: "Dry spells and darkness, all of it is painful for me: holy Communion, prayer, sermons, all of it, even telling Jesus that I love him is painful....I must cling to a life of faith. If I at least felt that Jesus loves me, my pain would be less, but he never says that to me" (VN, 32).

Some days, don't we seem to act like children who only do their homework to get the reward their mothers have promised to them for doing it rather than to please her? How can we speak of love—and even of pure love—if we only look for spiritual candy? Is it only our own satisfaction that counts? At the crossroads of our questions, we always return to the fundamental requirement to lose one's life. As Brother Charles says: "The more we embrace the cross, the more closely we clutch Jesus who is attached to it" (CB, 43).

If our Christianity is terribly demanding, it must not put forward a forbidding face. That would be contrary to what Christians are called to live. For Saint Paul's contemporaries, his preachings about the crucified Christ seemed to be utter foolishness. Nevertheless, Jesus' first teachings on earth spoke about happiness and enumerated blessings. Brother Charles, this austere religious whose meditations reflected the rigors of the gospel, was not a severe or unhappy man. All who encountered him praised his goodness and his smile: "He was very happy, it was undeniable, it was visible....His eyes were sparkling with calm and silent joy," said E. F. Gautier. Discovering joy, profound joy, when one has just lived through an act of total abandonment worse than a "blind jump into the dark," many Christians have had this experience: "I continue to find that I am too happy on this earth, not deserving of such happiness, not having sought it. I wanted to suffer something for God and the world."

Lord, may I always live in a state of self-abandonment, like a calm and trusting child. Even during the difficult times, you are there, Lord. Strength which comes from you pushes the limits of my possibilities aside and permits me to repeat: "No matter what you do with me, I thank you."

Lord, allow me also to think lovingly of my death. Its formidable character clouds my thinking and prevents me from classifying it with happy events. The child in its mother's womb fears the leap into the unknown, which, to him, represents birth. Those who love him call him to leave the warmth of his fragile comfort in order to obtain the fullness of life and the resplendence of the light. Am I always ready to hear a similar call: "Here comes my Spouse"?

Every day, do I add to the attentive acceptance of the present, the detachment of the one who is ready to leave it all behind at sunset? Lord, beyond the pain of departing, I must never have any doubts that you extend your arms to me and that the celebration is about to begin. Then, following in the footsteps of Abraham and Mary, I can only repeat: "Here I am, Lord," and if I am confident and have totally abandoned myself, Lord, I can add: "there is evidently no rush."

Let us join Brother Charles in these words: "Let us abandon ourselves. My God, you are there, I fear nothing, I bless you for everything because everything comes from you.... Everything that happens is permitted, prepared by, and given out by you for the greater good. Let us abandon ourselves" (QPR, 134).

REFLECTION QUESTIONS

Brother Charles lived his life in total abandonment to the will of Jesus. What does abandonment mean to you? Brother Charles says that "the more we embrace the cross, the more closely we clutch Jesus who is attached to it." How do you deal with your sense of aloneness and abandonment? Do you see these periods of inner suffering as a call to surrender to Jesus and allow him to live his passion in you?

DAY FIFTEEN

We Will Never Love Enough

FOCUS POINT

Love was at the center of Brother Charles's life, his great love for Jesus, and his desire to witness to Christ through loving those around him. Alone and isolated from other Christians, he had to put his life in trust and abandon it to Jesus. In the end, this was total love for Charles.

"Then he bowed his head and gave up his spirit" (Jn 19:30), says the Gospel. My Lord Jesus, you have died and died for us! If we truly had faith in that, we would want to die, die as martyrs. (...) The worst that man could make happen to us is that we perish in great torment; and, such a death, when accepted as conforming to your will and love, is a perfect grace...a thrice blessed imitation of you, my divine Jesus.

No matter what the motive is for them to kill us, if we in our soul accept this unjust and cruel death as a blessed gift from you, if we thank you for it as we would for a sweet grace...if we offer it as a sacrifice which is offered willingly, if we don't resist so that we can obey your words and follow your example...then, no matter what the motive is for killing us, we will die in pure love, and our death will be a sacrifice with a pleasant odor to you. And if it is not martyrdom in the strictest sense of the word as mankind judges it, then it would fit your judgment, and it would be a most perfect image of your death....For if, in this case, we haven't offered our blood for our faith, we would have offered it with all our heart and sacrificed it for your love (EDS, 193–194).

Our self-obliteration is the most powerful way that we have to unite ourselves with Jesus and to do good for souls: that is what Saint John of the Cross repeated in practically every line of his writings. When we can suffer and love, we can do a great deal; we can do more than we can do in this world. We can feel it when we suffer, we can't always feel it when we love and that causes even more suffering! But we know that we want to love, and to want to love is to love. We find that we don't love enough. It is true that we will never love enough, but the Good Lord knows with which clay he molded us, and he loves us more than a mother could love her child. He told us, he who doesn't lie, that he would never push away anyone who came to him (LMB, 251–252).

———

Lord Jesus, on Palm Sunday, toward four or five o'clock in the afternoon, you explained the significance of your impending death as the successful conclusion of your work. You say: "Very truly, I tell you, unless a grain of wheat falls into the earth and dies, it remains a single grain; but if it dies, it bears much fruit. Those who love their life lose it, and those who hate their life in this world will keep it for eternal life" (Jn 12:24–25).

Brother Charles was always convinced that he must die for his work to be fruitful. When he asked his correspondents for the support of their prayers, he often brought up this comparison to the grain of wheat: "Help me die so that I will bring fruit" (OS, 403). He, who so aspired to gather those around him and increase the numbers of his communities, not just in the Sahara but around the world (in Rome, in Bethany, and so on), saw his solitude in the same terms as the grain of wheat which has not died, but remains alone. "If the grain of wheat dies, it bears much fruit....I am not dead, I am also alone....Pray for my conversion so that, by dying, I will bear fruit" (OS, 399).

This law of fruitfulness, which is the cross, supports all apostolic activities: it is universal. The grain of wheat represents Christian life. We must die in order to bear fruit. It is not necessary to envision a heroic end, but only an "ordinary death." We are all called to carry our cross and "lose our life." For the past fourteen days that we have spent with Brother Charles, we have learned that everything points to this mystery of life which springs from death. The eucharistic liturgy proclaims: "Lord, by your death, you have given life to the world." When our turn comes, by taking communion in Jesus, each of us must die. Our death is achieved in thousands of ways: through detachment from worldly goods; through obedience to the Lord's calls and total self-abandonment to his will; through service to our brothers and sisters to the detriment of our peacefulness or our own love; through our persistent prayers during the darkest of our nights of faith or suffering....We do not choose the means, but we can generously accept them, through self-abandonment. Lord, when we hang the cross on our walls, we are reminded of your declaration of love which it symbolizes. When we welcome you into our lives, we are expressing, to the best of our ability, a loving response. When we contemplate on the Cavalries which appear in the midst of our lives, we also hear the joyous bells peal out in endless celebration of your Resurrection. This dual chant of the cross and the glory follows us in our daily lives.

Ever since Brother Charles, when he was in his hut in Nazareth, discovered the writings of Saint John of the Cross, he often cited a maxim which, in its own way, reiterates the law of the grain of wheat. In a letter, Brother Charles states it this way: "Pray so that I love the Cross, not for itself, but because it is the only way, the only path to glorify Jesus: 'the grain of wheat only bears fruit by dying,' and 'I, when I am lifted up from the earth, will draw all people to myself' (Jn 12:32). And as Saint John of the Cross remarked, it was at the time of his supreme annihilation, his death, that Jesus did the most good, that he saved the world" (OS, 48). This is what Brother Charles said in 1903 and, following that, I do not know how many times. He wrote it again on the day that he died, shortly before he felt in his flesh that the end was near.

Brother Charles strived to die like the grain of wheat, obscurely, in an ordinary way, but he also dreamed of a death which would imitate that of Jesus even more. He dreamed of a martyr's death. He wanted it for twenty years, he prepared for it, he wished for it for his future brothers. He made a prophetic description of it when he said: "Think that you must die like a martyr, stripped of everything, laid out on the ground, naked, unrecognizable, covered with wounds and blood, painfully and violently killed...and wish that it would happen to-day!" (VN, 35).

Such a spiritual state, far from being masochistic, is only understood through the will to imitate his beloved Lord Jesus and to take his teachings seriously. He wrote: "If you knew how much I want my poor, miserable life, which began so badly and is so empty, to end in the same way as Jesus spoke about at the Last Supper—that there is no greater love than to give one's life for someone you love. I am unworthy of it, but I want it so much!" (LMB, 102).

Day and night, Brother Charles contemplated his divine model and allowed himself to be guided by the instructions he was given, going by the maxim that "the degree of imitation is an indication of the amount of love." Just as Jesus, through his death, gave us "the greatest proof of love," for Brother Charles "to ask for, to want and, if it pleases God, to suffer martyrdom is to love Jesus with the greatest love" (DP, 75). And, in order to love, we must welcome the cross by renouncing our sense of self: "The only true love, the only one worthy of the name," says Brother Charles, "is the one by which we forget ourselves and forget everything in order to no longer want but one single thing, to no longer live but for one thing: the good of the Beloved" (CE, 91).

By this point we have come back to the first day when Jesus made the greatest commandment, love, superior to all limitations of the law. His listeners heard Jesus congratulating the scribe, declaring to him: "do this and you will live" (Lk 10:28). The gospel speaks to us even today. Lord Jesus, it is then to me that you address this precept: "do this," that is to say, "love God and love your neighbor." "Love God and your neighbor, love your neighbor so that, through this love, you can come to love God. These two loves cannot be separated:

to grow in one is to grow in the other" (LLM, 83). You will love, you command me, and you will live. Lord Jesus, what a magnificent program: to love is to live.

That is so because you have created us in the image of a living God who identifies himself with love. "God is love, and those who abide in love abide in God, and God abides in them" (1 Jn 4:16), says the epistle. Love, even if the cross must be the proof and sign of it, in the same way as you wanted it for yourself, Lord. The cross is the painful opposite of a burning love: blood and fire are the same color, the color of the insignia worn by Brother Charles. The heart, the emblem of love, is forever pierced by the cross. And love is stronger than death.

At the time of death, the last words always take on a moving significance. However, it seems, that from the moment he was tied up by his assailants, no words escaped from Brother Charles's lips, but he had left three letters on his table. The following are his last comments.

By a strange coincidence, he referred back to a time, six years earlier, when his spiritual father, on his death bed, had whispered his final words to him. In 1910, he wrote: "The mail just brought me the details about the last moments in the life of the one into whose hands I was converted twenty-four years ago and who has remained, since then, my beloved father. He was aware of everything right up until the end but could barely speak. His last words were: '*amabo numquam satis*' (I will never love enough) and 'we have value through what we love.' He was speaking to himself, having difficulty gathering his thoughts. These two phrases sum up his life" (LLM, 83).

On December 1, 1916, Brother Charles's hand was mysteriously guided to write these same words: "We will never love enough." His last message is a call to love and to love even more. Lord Jesus, when faced with these writings and this heroic death, I feel small and weak. I have the impression that it is an inaccessible ideal. Nevertheless, Brother Charles confided to us: "If I at least felt that Jesus loves me, but he never says it to me," and, before dying: "We don't always feel that we love...but we know that we want to love and wanting to love is to love." How he brings himself closer to me through his confidences!

Lord, I also want to love you, through the thousand actions of my daily life: by praying to you and praising you, since to pray is to love and to praise is to love; by accepting the will of the Father, since to obey is to love; by being poor through imitation and love; by constantly loving my brothers and sisters, since what I do to them, I also do to you....Perhaps, Lord, if we add it all up it doesn't amount to much. But you could do no less for me than the father of the prodigal.

REFLECTION QUESTIONS

We most likely will not live the style of life that Brother Charles lived. Yet his life teaches us a profound lesson of love. What are the ways you show your commitment to Christ? How do you experience the life of Jesus in yourself? What would you want to do differently in your life that would express the love of Jesus in a clearer way? What insights in the life and writings of Brother Charles have influenced you?

Bibliography

Bazin, René. *Charles de Foucauld: Hermit and Explorer.* New York: Benziger Bros., 1923.

Bodley, R. V. C. *The Warrior Saint.* Boston: Little, Brown, 1953.

Carrouges, Michel. *Soldier of the Spirit: The Life of Charles de Foucauld.* New York: Putnam, 1956.

Castillon du Perron, Marguerite. *Charles de Foucauld.* Paris: B. Brasset, 1982.

Freemantle, Anne Jackson. *Desert Calling.* New York: Holt, 1949.

Gorrée, George. *Memories of Charles de Foucauld: Explorer and Hermit, Seen in His Letters.* London: Burns, Oates & Washbourne, Ltd., 1938.

Hamilton, Elizabeth. *The Desert My Dwelling Place: A Study of Charles de Foucauld.* London: Hodder & Stoughton, 1968.

Lepetit, Charles. *Two Dancers in the Desert: The Life of Charles de Foucauld.* Maryknoll, N.Y.: Orbis Books, 1984.

Preminger, Marion Mill. *The Sands of Tamanrasset: The Story of Charles de Foucauld.* New York: Hawthorn Books, 1961.

Six, Jean-François. *Spiritual Autobiography of Charles de Foucauld.* New York: P. J. Kennedy, 1964.

————. *Witness in the Desert: The Life of Charles de Foucauld.* New York: Macmillan, 1965.

Trouncer, Margaret. *Charles de Foucauld.* London: G. G. Harrap, 1972.